Voices

of

Teachers

Report of a Survey on Social Studies

National Commission on Social Studies in the Schools

A joint project of the
American Historical Association
Carnegie Foundation for the Advancement of Teaching
National Council for the Social Studies
Organization of American Historians

KENDALL/HUNT PUBLISHING COMPANY
2460 Kerper Boulevard   P.O. Box 539   Dubuque, Iowa 52004-0539

*The development and publication of this booklet was made possible by grants from The
Rockefeller Foundation, the National Geographic Society Education Foundation, the
Carnegie Corporation of New York, the John D. and Catherine T. MacArthur Founda-
tion, and by the four founding organizations; however, the staff of the National
Commission on Social Studies in the Schools is solely responsible for its content.*

Editorial Staff on this publication:

David Jenness, Scholar in Residence;
Mary E. Kennedy, Director, Adviser-Responder Schools Network;
Fay D. Metcalf, Executive Director, National Commission on Social Studies in the Schools
Salvatore J. Natoli, Director of Publications, National Council for the Social Studies

Layout and design: Dan Kaufman, Coordinator of Desktop Publishing, National Council for the Social Studies

Table of Contents

Foreword

Concern over the lack of clarity and agreement in social studies, the lack of coherence in history, geography, and the social sciences at all education levels, and the many complex challenges faced by the schools led the governing bodies of the American Historical Association, in 1984, and National Council for the Social Studies, in 1985, to call for a national commission to determine goals and priorities and to recommend ways and means for re-ordering and strengthening the curriculum and the teaching of social studies in the schools. In December 1985 these two organizations agreed to join forces in a combined effort, and inaugurated a project to establish the National Commission on Social Studies in the Schools. The Carnegie Foundation for the Advancement of Teaching and the Organization of American Historians joined the coalition a few months later.

Because social studies draws on all the social sciences, the founding organizations extended invitations to all the relevant professional organizations to join the enterprise. In addition, invitations were issued to teachers, administrators, and members of the concerned public. Since 1985, the National Commission consulted over 80 organizations concerned with education who offered advice and encouragement to the Commission in its work. The inauguration of the National Commission meant that, for the first time in more than 50 years, all major relevant educational organizations and representative groups were united in a coalition dedicated to the reform of that vital portion of the education of the young.

The Executive Committee organized itself in early 1986 and took steps to organize the full Commission and its staff. The Commission held its first plenary meeting in November 1987. During the next three years, the National Commission examined the content and effectiveness of instruction in our elementary and secondary schools, the goals of such studies, and the priorities in the field. It charged its Curriculum Task Force to make recommendations for reform, and report to the Commission. The Task Force responded with its November 1989 report, *Charting a Course: Social Studies for the 21st Century*,[1] which the Commission, in its last act, printed and distributed across the United States. The report takes a bold stand on what actually needs to be taught in K-12 social studies courses.

As the Commission and its Task Force undertook their tasks, they realized that reform of social studies was hindered by not only a lack of agreement on what should be done in the classroom, but also by a failure to understand what had been recommended, and accomplished or not accomplished, in the past. All too little was known of the cumulative experience of the various social studies reform movements during the past 75 years or of how those reform movements had played themselves out in classrooms across the country. To obtain this important information, the Commission took two steps: it called upon their fellow Commissioner David Jenness to prepare a book-length study of the history of the social studies movements, with particular attention to the efforts of the disciplines at various stages to influence and shape social studies in the schools,[2] and it established the Advisor-Responder (AR) Network of Schools to find out from teachers themselves what they are currently doing in the classroom and what they believe ought to be done in the future. This report summarizes some of the more interesting findings from the teachers involved in the Network.

The Commission extends it heartfelt thanks to the staff for undertaking this necessary and difficult task. In particular we wish to thank Mary Kennedy, Director of the AR schools' project, for her untiring efforts in managing the project; Marina Reichert-Erickson who managed data analysis and Judith Torney-Purta who provided advice as well as computer services; part-time research associates Joseph Hartlaub and Ned Hartfiel who, along with volunteer current and former teachers Paul Burke, Billie Day, Thomas R. Averett, John Driscoll, Lelia Ermath, Richard Galvin, Brigette K. Lavey, Jerry Marquis, Robert Anderman, Dennis Cochran, Deborah Drucker, Brian Whitmer, Erich Wilson, and Joseph La Blanc, spent endless hours organizing and summarizing data; David Jenness, Scholar in Residence, for his help in making sense of the vast quantities of collected data; and Executive Director Fay Metcalf for her able assistance in this, as well as in all other tasks, of the National Commission on Social Studies in the Schools. Finally, we wish to pay special tribute to the teachers who made the project possible. They spent many hours answering the several surveys and responding to requests for advice on many aspects of the Commission's work. Our children are in good hands with these dedicated educators; we hope that the efforts of the Commission will help make such conditions available to all our nation's young people.

Arthur S. Link, President of the Commission; George Henry Davis '86 Professor of History, Princeton University; former President of the American Historical Association, the Organization of American Historians, and the Southern Historical Association

Ernest L. Boyer, Vice-President of the Commission; President of the Carnegie Foundation for the Advancement of Teaching; former U. S. Commissioner of Education

Stanley N. Katz, Executive Committee Liaison for the Commission; President of the American Council of Learned Societies; former President of the Organization of American Historians

---

[1] Ordering information may be found on the inside back cover of this publication.

[2] David Jenness, *Making Sense of Social Studies*, New York: Macmillan Publishing Company, 1990. Ordering information may be found on the inside of the back cover.

National Commission on Social Studies in the Schools
Adviser-Responder Schools

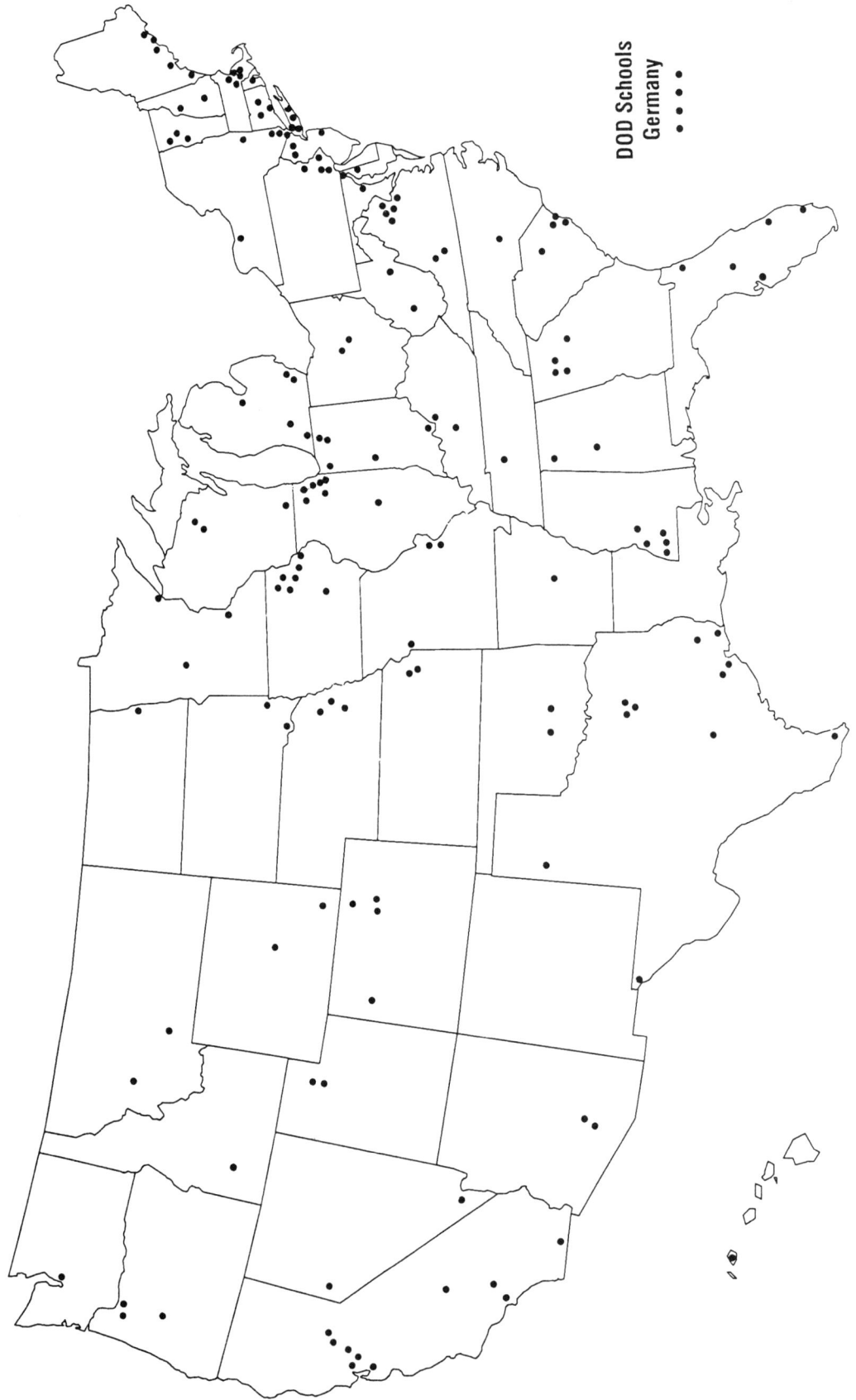

DOD Schools
Germany

1. How the Study Came About

Established in 1986 as a joint project of the American Historical Association, the Carnegie Foundation for the Advancement of Teaching, the National Council for the Social Studies, and the Organization of American Historians, the **National Commission on Social Studies in the Schools** was charged with examining the current status of social studies and to make recommendations for needed change. The Report of its 14-member Curriculum Task Force, *Charting A Course: Social Studies for the 21st Century*, was published in the fall of 1989.[1] A book-length analysis of the historical and current status of the field, *Making Sense of Social Studies*, by David Jenness, will appear in September 1990.[2]

The Adviser-Responder (A-R) School Network was organized early in the life of the Commission, as a mechanism for a large number of teachers to have direct opportunity to influence its work. While the Commission itself included 7 practicing teachers and 12 others who had begun their careers as teachers, the Commissioners believed it important to hear from social studies teachers across the country. Following a suggestion made by Jim Kraft, a teacher from Wausau, Wisconsin, potential volunteers were informed about the proposed network at professional meetings and through articles in social studies journals. In the end, some 777 teachers chose to serve as Adviser-Responders.

As their name suggests, the A-R teachers were asked to provide the Commission and its committees or task forces with information and to respond critically to the work of the Commission at various stages.

With regard to providing information, over a period of 20 months, five questionnaires, constructed by staff of the National Commission, were sent to these teachers. The first, called the *Community Profile* (CP), went to contact persons in schools or districts where one or more individuals had expressed interest in the network. These individuals (in many cases, the person who had made the initial contact) completed the questionnaire, which asked for basic data on the school or system, the community in which it was located, and its curricular and professional characteristics, on behalf of the group. (In cases where we had only one respondent from a school or district, she or he was of course the contact person.) The contact person recruited other teachers to respond, individually, to the later questionnaires, and often acted as the liaison for distribution and for return of those questionnaires. The subsequent questionnaires were: a *Teacher Profile* (TP), *Questionnaire A* on curriculum design and emphasis, *Questionnaire B* on approaches to teaching, and a final questionnaire dealing with the impact of contests, national projects, and other extracurricular activities on the teaching and learning of social studies. This Report deals with the first four questionnaires. A report on the last will be published in article form at a later time.

Incoming responses from the several questionnaires provided important data to the Curriculum Task Force (CTF) as it considered, debated, and refined its report, *Charting A Course*. The idea was not for the opinions and preferences of the A-R teachers to determine the scope or nature of the Curriculum Task Force Report—which represents only the considered judgments of its members, arrived at through a committee process—but for knowledge and opinions from this source to be available to the CTF members in the course of their work. The CTF found this documentation of present practices, concerns, and opinions invaluable in framing and refining their own deliberations, since all too often such deliberative groups move toward recommendations based on questionable assumptions about present reality. It was particularly useful for the Task Force to be able to determine not only the overall weight of opinion on many points (that is, what might be obtained from a simple opinion poll), but to discern the dimensions of and arguments for (and against) well-articulated minority positions.

Fulfilling their role as advisers (in addition to responding to questionnaires), many of the A-R teachers took the opportunity to write long letters and position papers and to make thoughtful comments on several drafts of the Task Force's report. Although, as stated, the Task Force ultimately spoke only for itself, *Charting A Course* is a better document for such periodic assessment from teachers. In turn, the document should be especially meaningful to those teachers who followed and contributed to the process of its drafting.

The present research report, *Voices of Teachers*, is a fuller and more thoroughly analyzed version of the data from the four questionnaires—the information that had been relayed to the Curriculum Task Force in an ongoing and fairly informal fashion. For example, while the Task Force examined many responses for their verbatim wording and had frequency tables for the distributions of responses to the various questions, the present report utilized computer cross-tabulations prepared for us by statistical consultant, Marina Reichhart-Erickson.

This report is the work of National Commission staff:

Mary E. Kennedy, Director, Adviser-Responder Schools Network

David Jenness, Scholar in Residence

Fay D. Metcalf, Executive Director

Joseph Hartlaub and **Ned Hartfiel**, Research Assistants

The National Commission makes available this report because of the inherent interest and possible value of these data in present discussions of social studies in the American schools. As educational studies go, this is a fairly large-scale exploration of one curriculum area. It involves a large number of questions, and data gathered from many individuals. The study was initiated and conducted by experienced persons, was sponsored by highly reputable organizations, and earned the participation of respondents who clearly took it seriously. As such, the results deserve careful attention.

It is extremely important, however, to emphasize the real limitations of the study. As it turned out, the Adviser-Responder teachers who participated were fairly representative, descriptively speaking, of geographic regions, of types of schools, and of ethnic and economic communities in the U.S. as a whole. In some respects, since a good national description of *social studies teachers* does not exist, our study population gives the only known current description. This does not mean, however, that this study provides a "true" picture. There are several reasons for this caution. The A-R teachers, though numerous, were self-selected. Volunteers do tend to be the vanguard, the particularly dedicated teachers across the nation who care most deeply about their profession and who want to do what they can to improve the quality of education in their communities. Research experience and our own judgment of our study population suggests that much run-of-the-mill practice is not reflected in these results. Second, it is well established that the answers and judgments one obtains from questionnaire surveys, particularly in a complex or specialized field, depend considerably on how and when the questions are put: on their wording, their order, their implications, and many related factors. Our questionnaires were not pre-tested, nor have they been used in settings other than the intended one, nor were alternative forms of these questionnaires tried. Thus we cannot make any assessment of how substantial any of these "questionnaire effects" may be.

Third, our study took place at a time of considerable public and professional concern with the curriculum and with teaching, reflected in the presence of other studies, other commissions, and the like. Some of our respondents, in some of their responses, may have been listening to questions other than ours, and may have been speaking to an audience beyond what we intended. Some may have given answers they thought they should give, while others may have given answers that they particularly wanted to have carry the day. (To some degree, the relatively large number in the study population will work against the latter.) Fourth, the A-R teachers were asked to spend a very large amount of time. Not only were they asked to complete five lengthy questionnaires, but we know that some groups of respondents met frequently to discuss the study, assess drafts of *Charting A Course*, and so on. Not surprisingly, as the questionnaires kept arriving, and as they became more and more difficult to fill out—calling for more and more evaluative and judgmental responses—the number of completed questionnaires dropped. Those who completed Questionnaires A and B were only a subset of those originally involved; this could conceivably mean that they were a different study group (p. 37).

For all these reasons, we have been careful to avoid assigning statistical significance to any of our results; we have chosen to report the raw frequencies or simple percentages; we refer to our respondents as "the study group" rather than as "the sample" (since a sample of which "population" is not clear); and we have tried to be modest in the kinds of inferences and conclusions we draw.[3]

To repeat, however: we know of no comparable information about American social studies as of about 1990. Thanks to the teachers themselves, in this Commission at least, voices from the classroom are heard. We express great appreciation to these teachers, and hope that the results of this study will be useful to them as well as to a larger audience.

2. What the Teachers Are Saying

Based on their responses to four questionnaires, the social studies teachers in our Adviser-Responder Network show substantial agreement on six main principles:

1.   Use history and geography as the central core of instruction
2.   Relate knowledge of the past to present-day issues and changes in the modern world
3.   Define and then limit the "facts" that must be taught, so that it is possible for students to investigate the essential subject matter in depth
4.   Tie the necessary facts and concepts of the social studies together with deeper inquiry by means of "big ideas," drawn from a number of disciplines and branches of knowledge, from a variety of cultures, and from both traditional and contemporary thinking
5.   Develop specific cognitive skills so that students can become active, lifelong learners
6.   Take as the overriding general purpose of social studies the goal of producing young Americans knowledgeable about and dedicated to their country's democratic values and prepared to participate effectively as citizens in the world.

Principle 1

Social studies should center in the study of the historical and geographical processes that have shaped today's world. To this framework should be related content and concepts from the other social sciences, the humanities and arts, and the sciences. Most teachers, by far, emphasized the need for more, but better and more selective, instruction in these core subjects. Other detailed social science knowledge can in most respects be correlated with a grasp of this essential subject matter.

Students, as citizens of the United States in the 21st century, must have knowledge of historical, geographical, economic, religious, political, social, and cultural developments of their own local and national environment. However, it is most important that they also have this kind of knowledge about the rest of the world—for example, about the governments and laws of other societies as well as their own, and about the humanistic heritage of the world.

There are, among the A-R teachers, two minority views. One, held by a relatively small number of teachers, but held forcefully, is that social studies education should deal more with the present than with the past, and more with current issues than past events. For them, the individual approaches of the social sciences warrant careful and formal explication.

The other minority view is that none of the disciplines should be taught separately, but that history, geography, the other social sciences, the arts, humanities, and sciences should be integrated wherever possible, at all levels. Careful reading of the comments along these lines reveals little disagreement with the majority opinion in terms of principles, but a difference in curriculum organization and pedagogy—e.g., interdisciplinary team teaching or the eschewing of traditional textbooks.

I believe social studies is divided into three broad categories, including history-geography at the core or hub, with humanities and other social science disciplines as supporting axles into the hub of history and geography. The humanities provide the aesthetic link that engages students' imaginations, and the other social sciences broaden the context with appropriate information and concepts. (Middle Level Teacher, California)

I have always believed that too much time and attention in almost every social studies class is on the past. I believe the greatest improvement teachers can make in every course in the social studies would be to teach the present with the same degree of understanding and interest as they do the American Revolution. (Secondary Teacher, Louisiana)

Interdisciplinary teaching as well as group projects would help each student grow and develop skills. The emphasis on any 'ideal' or model should include basic skills in the content areas and a perspective of the earth as a global community that is all interrelated. (Secondary teacher, Vermont)

Principle 2

Most A-R teachers believe that it is within the historical-geographical framework that students should learn about and analyze contemporary issues. They think that it is critical that students be knowledgeable about such issues, that they form opinions and take positions on controversial questions, but that they examine these in a historical-geographical context. The rigorous selection of what necessary "facts" to teach in traditional courses is emphasized as being *in the service of* dealing with the complexities of present-day life. Thus a curriculum which never addresses the history of the world (other than Europe and North America), recent political events, foreign cultures of current importance, or the phenomena of international economics is inadequate. This principle holds, moreover, at each level of teaching, not simply for electives in the last years.

As suggested above (Principle 1), a minority of teachers believe that the curriculum must *begin* from a consideration of what is relevant and necessary knowledge in today's world. These teachers are not opposed to the history-geography framework, but believe that the selection of material and emphases depends more on an estimate of what the world will be like in the future, a world which today's students will inhabit, than on what previous generations experienced.

Principle 3

Adviser-Responder teachers generally report that the present curriculum is extremely difficult to complete given time constraints. It is in this area that teachers most often cite a need for the contribution of outside groups—from scholarly organizations to civic groups—for guidance. They do not, however, want such groups to nominate *more content*, but to make clear which facts and concepts they consider crucial—and, even more, in what areas of knowledge and inquiry they believe students need to be encouraged to explore on their own. Many teachers see a trend toward a particular kind of standardized achievement testing as part of the problem—the kind that puts a premium on the possession of discrete bits of "knowledge." Almost all teachers who wrote extensive comments on these issues said, in one way or another, that the important choices involve knowing when to teach, when to facilitate students' own learning; what to include, and what to drop. That these are not necessarily forced choices is suggested in their comments dealing with the following principle.

Principle 4

Network teachers stress the importance of a curriculum that is alert to connections among the disciplines and that builds on big ideas. This is closely related, of course, to the question of what to leave out, and how to break down "coverage" of subject matter for its own sake. Almost unanimously, teachers agree that depth is better than coverage for the sake of coverage. The hard choices about what are the "big ideas" involve the traditional interrelationships among the social sciences, but just as often involve the other branches of knowledge as well. Casting widely for ideas and concepts, however, can be as superficial as the "endless mentioning" of facts. Simply touching on the ideas of great thinkers in science or the established traditions of the humanities can amount to a kind of facile slide show.

A personal bias is that every social studies teacher use a current-events-based vehicle to provide thinking and learning skills, to provide much of the basic knowledge necessary for knowledgeable students, and to provide relevance and reality in the social studies classroom. (Middle Level Teacher, Colorado)

Social studies has got to find a sense of direction. Educators have got to decide what are the fundamental experiences that humans have encountered throughout the centuries and use them as the foundation. (Elementary Teacher, Connecticut)

I see a well-articulated curriculum much like a special continuum where little is repeated, but much is reinforced by new examples and expressions...Students should learn something each day that they did not know before, regardless of their prior knowledge. (Secondary Teacher, California)

Right now I am pleased with the themes we are using in our American Studies (humanities) course: diversity, identity, law, and progress. Our course is fitting so well around those organizing themes (in both history and literature). (Secondary Teacher, Illinois)

The principal qualification here is the very evident, all-pervasive anxiety about time. Not instructional time per se, but time for the teachers to "make the connections" and time for the students to appreciate and explore those connections. Ancillary to the former is some concern with better texts and materials, especially in world history and geography. A part of the latter is freedom (for the student as well as the teacher) from the lock-step routine, freedom to *not* teach every unit in the text, freedom to examine, in class, what is happening in the everyday world. Many of the A-R teachers individually report that they are best, as teachers, at "making the connections," but they do this in and around the defined curriculum, not as part of it.

Principle 5

In most respects, teachers believe that for students to be effective lifelong learners, such inquiry must be discipline-based. There must be enough knowledge of the fundamental concerns, facts, and methods in the various subject areas for students to understand the "rules of the game" as they explore further. Thus, even those who most emphasize a history-geography core stress that understanding of legal or economic or cultural concepts must be in the terms appropriate to those fields.

Beyond this conviction are more general concerns, very strongly worded in A-R teachers' comments, for instilling solid reading and writing skills; the ability to find and make use of information in later life (media, libraries, graphic and data resources, and community and civic institutions); critical thinking skills (analyzing, drawing inferences, weighing likelihoods, recognizing interrelationships, synthesizing data, and using appropriate procedures in making decisions). Some teachers lay special emphasis on "skills" that involve human relations, group processes, cooperative learning, and debate, discussion, and decisions in public arenas. These latter abilities are directly relevant to the final proposition on which most teachers place emphasis.

Principle 6

The teachers' descriptions of good citizenship fall into three categories: informed participation in government; concern with fellow human beings by an enlightened view of history, social life, and institutions; and action based on moral and ethical values. Good citizenship values American democratic traditions, knows and celebrates the strengths of our society, recognizes its problems, and assumes active efforts toward maintaining the system while working for change. However, many or most of those who wrote extended comments on citizenship made it clear that there are several levels or perimeters involved: from responsible involvement with immediate groups and institutions locally, to enlightened political action on the state and national level, and then to a commitment to global betterment.

It is striking how so many respondents, from different educational backgrounds, teaching at different levels in very different milieux, and using different lines of argument, arrive at this same general conclusion. This principle transcends preferences and reasoning about the curriculum as such. This degree of consensus is perhaps misleading. It is not clear, in this study, what specific set or sequence of content, which knowledge-based skills, are needed for effective citizenship. How much of what kind of history? government? economics? how much training in discussion and debate? independent

It behooves the social studies teacher to give students many opportunities to choose the relevant from the irrelevant, and to make choices based on accurate information. They must be able to interpret the opinions of leaders, data, and other sources of information. They need to be able to temper their own opinions to avoid confrontations. Our world is so small that it sometimes seems we are like a 'pot ready to boil over.' Only cool heads and positive thinkers will be able to maintain the American way of life. The adults of tomorrow must be able to discern the factual from opinion and to make wise decisions. There will always be dissenters, but cool, logical thinkers must prevail! (Elementary Teacher, South Carolina)

———

Effective social studies instruction has to be instruction for the well-informed citizen. However, this informed citizen must have a base in U.S. History and awareness of global interests and cultural differences. (Middle Level Teacher, reading? information-gathering? public service? The details are largely missing in the tables and discussion that follow. The general goal is held so much in common that the pathways to it go untraced.

Conclusion

We note, running through the questionnaire responses in general, a consistent difference between the ways in which our teachers respond to questions about *existing arrangements*—essential content, courses, present classroom and school practices—and their comments about the *ideal spirit and tone of the enterprise*. We have focussed upon this contrast in Section 5 of this Report, but the differences run through all the data. Since this is a matter of some importance in current policy debates, we emphasize that much depends, in any educational inquiry, on what questions are asked and how they are phrased. Much depends also on whether teachers are addressing what is or what might be.

To take the most obvious example, the same teachers who (as a group) endorse a formal curriculum of a few core subjects, tightly interrelated, also speak with some passion in their additional comments for educating students in what seem to be the topics of cultural anthropology, comparative human geography, human-environmental interactions, international economics, the philosophy and sociology of science, and other large, often inherently interdisciplinary, ways of thinking. A careful reader may conclude that, in the curriculum, basic content is regarded as necessary but not sufficient.

The same is true, even more so, in our teachers' comments on the essence and extent of citizenship, the commitment to global stewardship, and the desire for students to be active learners on a lifelong basis. In studies of what—beyond factual mastery—public education is *for*, a degree of disjunction between ends and means has always been evident. More than 50 years after Charles A. Beard wrote *A Charter for the Social Sciences in the Schools*, for the 1930s Commission on the Social Studies, little has changed. As Beard said then, "Instruction in social studies is conditioned by the spirit and letter of scholarship, by the realities and ideas of the society in which it is carried on, and by the nature and limitations of the teaching process at the various grade levels across which it is distributed."[4]

What has changed since the 1930s is the nature of the school population—its size and ethnic composition; the nature of the experiences the students bring with them to the classroom —reflecting newer forms of information and communication; and the sense today of being part of a more complex and interdependent world.

As a student of history, it is apparent to me that the greatest problem we could face as a nation is public apathy to issues that confront us or will confront us in the future. Therefore, I want my social studies program to teach kids how to assume a role in our nation's political, social, and economic structure and continue to be active participants in the democratic process. I want my students to leave my class with a sense of justice and open mindedness and a desire to participate as active citizens. (Secondary Teacher, Missouri)

3. Present Practices and Preferences

Characteristics of the Respondents

Since the Adviser-Responder Schools in our study were self-selected, it is particularly important to describe what we know about the schools and teachers who participated.

On page VI is a map and list showing the location of A-R systems participating. Although in this report we often use the term "A-R schools," the location of our teacher respondents and the educational entities they represent is complex. All told, about 777 individual teachers participated in the study. They came from 216 separate educational systems. A "system" was in some cases a single school—the only school in a particular district that participated in the study. In other cases, the "system" was represented by more than one school. Out of our 216 distinct systems, 127 are single-school systems (for our study), and 89 involve more than one school. (About 321 individual schools participated, all told.)[5]

The geographical distribution of our A-R systems is shown below, and is compared to the sectional distribution of the total U.S. population.[6] Some dots on the map on p. xx represent more than one system, and four of the systems were U.S. army base schools in West Germany. Our distribution of systems is generally like that of the U.S. population; in our study, the Central and Mountain regions were slightly overrepresented.

Of 216 systems, 186 were public educational entities; 9 were parochial; 17 were independent (nonreligious); and 4 were unclassifiable in these terms. In this study we have not broken down data in terms of a public/nonpublic distinction.

Of 212 classifiable systems, the distribution of Urban, Rural-Small Town, and Suburban is seen in Figure 3. (Within the Rural-Small Town category, 26 systems were small town, 20 rural, and 8 intermediate.)

The teachers in our network work in about 321 individual schools. The *schools* and the *teachers* are divided among Elementary, Middle, and Secondary as follows:[7]

	Teaching Level			
	Elementary	Middle	Secondary	Total
No. of Schools	82	101	138	321
No. of Teachers	175	223	379	777
No. of Teachers (%)	22.5%	28.7%	48.7%	100%

School size as follows:

No. of Students (range)	176-860	75-1800	62-3600	
Mean No. of Students	470	738	1208	

Distribution of Adviser-Responder Schools

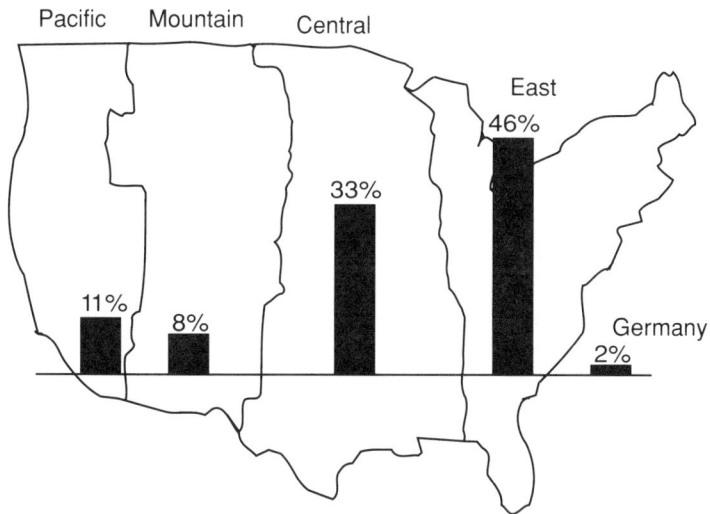

Distribution of U.S. Population

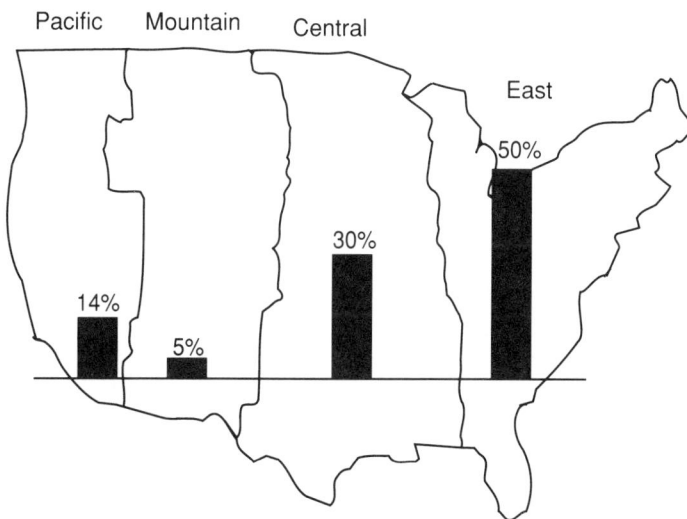

Figure 2

Community Profile

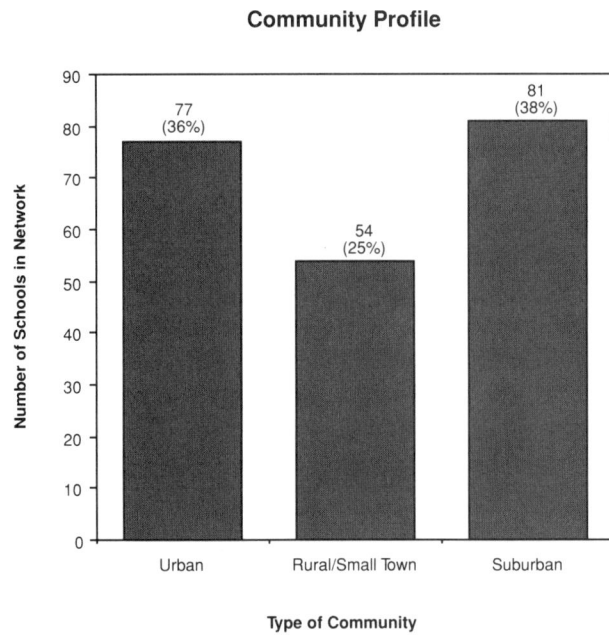

Figure 3

We estimate the total school population represented by our A-R schools as about 187,000; the total school population in their systems, about 3 million (excluding New York City schools).

One way of estimating the grade levels at which our teachers work is to ask them the *lowest* grade level at which they teach. This is shown in the figure below.

**Grade Level Taught by A-R Teachers
Shown by Lowest Grade Level Taught**

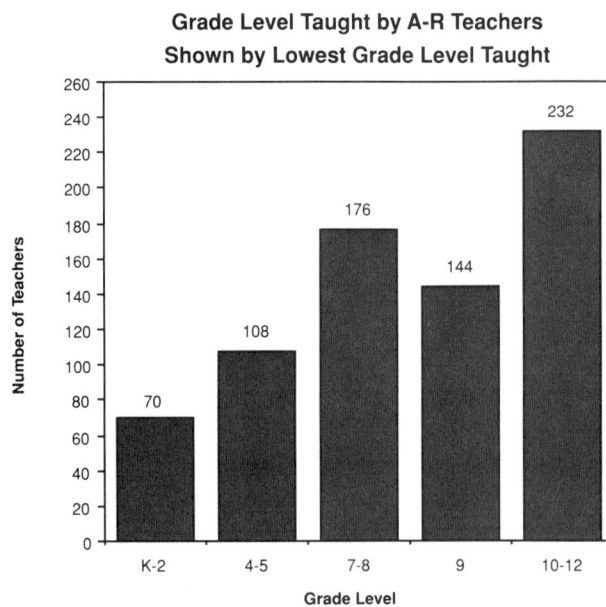

Figure 4

In our data, virtually no teachers *begin* teaching at grade 3 or grade 6. Since few teachers *begin* teaching at grade 11 or 12, it is a reasonable inference (supported by other evidence) that more secondary schools begin with grade 10 than with grade 9: another way of saying this is that some who *begin* teaching in grade 7 or 8 also teach grade 9, in a middle school or junior high school configuration.

We asked respondents completing the Community Profile questionnaire to indicate the ethnic make-up of their schools and systems. The results proved difficult to interpret. "Hispanics" were counted as White in some tallies, as Minority in others, and Asian and Pacific-origin students were also classified in various ways. In addition, great extremes were evident: an A-R school in Texas reporting 95% Hispanic, 5% White (Anglo); a school in Mississippi reporting 75% Black, 25% White; a school in New York City reporting 60% White (including Hispanic), 30% Asian, and 10% Black. In terms of the respondents' own classification, there was considerable difference between larger and smaller school systems:

Ethnic Distribution in A-R Schools (%s)

150 School Systems With Over 2,000 Students

Asian	Black	Hispanic	Indian/ Alaskan	White	Other
3.2	17.0	7.3	.7	71.5	.4

32 School Systems With Under 2,000 Students

Asian	Black	Hispanic	Indian/ Alaskan	White	Other
2.4	3.1	5.0	.8	88.6	.2

We were more confident about the interpretation of the socio-economic status of *school community* (i.e., the town or district, not the in-school population), as provided by A-R respondents than about ethnic composition.[8] "Mixed" was the most common (39%) descriptor (in this usage, almost always indicating a combination of middle class, lower middle class, and deprived), followed by middle class(30%), lower middle class/deprived(19%), and affluent(12%).

Self-Reported Economic Status

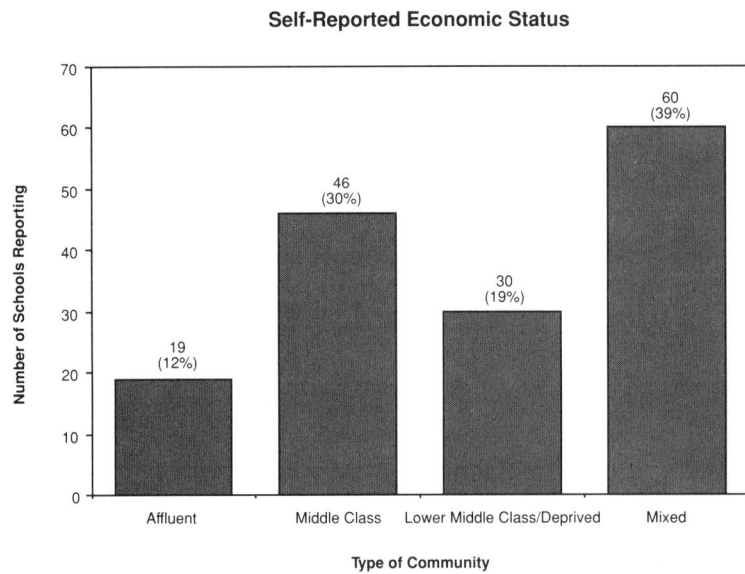

Figure 5

We now turn to reporting data gathered from the four questionnaires administered in this study. (See p. 1.)

Existing Curriculum and Organization

◆   CP1   [Community Profile] Title and grade level of social studies courses required in your district.

◆   CP2   How are requirements determined?

We found it impossible to summarize the answers to CP1 in any very meaningful way. The *titles* of instructional units vary widely from system to system and from educational level to level. If we had asked respondents to name the *subject matter* of courses, the replies might have been more orderly. There was also evident a pervasive and understandable confusion about the meaning of "required"—the legal force of a requirement, the presence of a "requirement" in some but not all schools in a district, or for some but not all students. Finally, some elements in a curriculum are "required" but do not amount to separate courses: e.g., instruction in civic participation, or free enterprise economics.

In rough summary, what the teachers perceive as requirements are, in rank order: U.S. history, state history, and geography—the last often present under other names or as part of other courses.

An analysis of the teachers' reports of the source of "requirements" in their districts is as follows:

Systems		
	No.	Percent
State mandates	36	19.8
School board	20	11.0
Faculty, department	7	3.9
Combination	119	65.3

This result is consistent with what is reported in the literature about course requirements, which are under multiple levels or kinds of determination.[9]

◆   CP3   How many minutes per week of social studies is required?

Teachers are good informants on this aspect of the curriculum (taking "required" in their own definition). (Cf TP3)

Time Required for Social Studies (per week)				
Level	Elementary		Middle	Secondary
	K-3	4-6		
No. of schools	29	101	131	150
Average hours per week	1.9	3.0	4.0	4.2

With regard to K-3 and 4-6, these results are close to national averages as reported in careful studies in 1977 by the National Science Foundation. (Similar national censuses for higher grade levels are lacking.) There is no evidence here that our A-R respondents are unusually favored or burdened, in terms of teaching time available for social studies.

◆   CP4   What *electives* are offered and approximately how many students take these electives each year?

Of the 153 systems for which we have good answers, 20 do not offer electives in social studies. (The 20 are not concentrated at the elementary or middle school levels, but are among the smallest schools.) Of these 133, in 94 cases we do not know whether the electives offered are the same across individual schools, or different: in 62 of 94 cases (66%), electives vary from school to school, representing school-based choice.

In the 133 systems, 139 separate course or content areas were cited, referring to 570 separate course offerings. The ratio of 139:570 has no clear significance. Many elective course titles (like some required course titles) are chosen to appeal to students, express a special emphasis (e.g., Conflicts in American Society), reflect the use of a particular textbook (e.g., Street Law), or distinguish between similar offerings (e.g., AP European History as distinct from European History); thus there will be a relatively high ratio of titles to course areas. Conversely, some frequently used titles (e.g., "American Problems") may conceal a wide diversity of subjects and emphases; thus the ratio will be lower. Ignoring these complexities, the range of electives titles can be collapsed to some fairly stable content categories, as follows (based on 534 of the 570 named courses):

Content Area of Electives Offered

	Number of Courses Categorized	Percent of Courses Categorized
Behavioral Sciences	194	36
History	112	21
Economics	63	12
Government	46	9
Law	36	7
International Studies	36	7
Regional Studies	29	5
U.S. Studies	18	3
Total	534	100
[36 uncategorized]		

In these tabulations, Regional Studies refers to world regions, generally treated in an interdisciplinary way (Latin America, Middle East, et al.), whereas International Studies refers to world or global subject matters, usually taught from a predominantly political science, world affairs/foreign policy, or geopolitical point of view. U.S. Studies is predominantly organized around current issues and problems. Government is centered on U.S. institutions and processes. Economics as a course is largely discipline-based (as opposed to personal or consumer economics). In Behavioral Sciences, psychology and sociology are about equally well represented, with anthropology far less frequent. Among History electives, world history, American history, and European history are about equally common at the top of a long list of titles (ranging from Afro-American history to Civil War history to Russian history), and Advanced Placement courses are fairly frequent.

It is interesting to note the relationship of frequency of *electives* in a curriculum area and the extent to which the subjects are typically *required* at the secondary level. Some history is almost always required there, and government and economics are sometimes required. Behavioral science is almost never required. A reasonable conclusion is that electives offered track student demand (or perceived need): i.e., that there is demand for behavioral science instruction, and to a lesser extent courses in international and regional studies, even though they are not a part of the "set" curriculum; and demand for history, and to a lesser extent government and economics, *over and above* what is required. Some subjects—e.g., anthropology or comparative religion—are so infrequent that their presence in the curriculum probably indicates the interests of particular teachers on the faculty.

◆ CP6(a)   How are decisions made about changing social studies curriculum?

The responses to this question were analyzed in terms of where—at what level—decisions were made.

Level of Decision-Making

	No. of systems	Percent
Individual teachers	10	6
Local school	31	17
School district	44	25
State agency	17	10
Combination of above	76	43
Total	178	100

[No response 9]

◆ CP6(b)   Is there a school, district, or state curriculum committee? What is its function?

Composition of Curriculum Committees

	No. of systems
State-level committee only	31
District and state combined	9
District committee only	54
District and school combined	31
School committee only	13
School and district and state	15
School and state	5
Total	158

[No response 20]

In analyzing the responses to CP6(a) and 6(b) together, it was clear that there is a layering and dispersion of curriculum authority in terms of practical decision-making, but one which *centers* at the district level with considerable input from individual schools. Only in certain states are curriculum decisions made centrally. Unless top-down state authority pre-empts the process, districts seem to gather and weigh the results of deliberations at the school level and arrive at an over-all course of action (sometimes under the leadership of a curriculum specialist from the state or a nearby university).[10]

◆ CP6(c)   Do teachers write new course materials?

In more than 90 percent of the systems for which responses were obtained, teachers did so. (See CP8.)

◆ CP6(d)   Does the school system provide inservice training for teachers preparing new materials/courses? (Cf CP9)

	No. of systems	Percent
Yes	105	59
No	59	33
Sometimes	15	8
Total	179	100

[No response 8]

◆ CP7   Are any type of standardized social studies tests mandated by the school or school district? How are the results of standardized tests used?

This question proved defective. As mentioned above, most teachers use "mandated" in this context to mean prescribed (not necessarily formally) or the norm in their system; this was the sense in which the question was intended. Some respondents took "mandated" to mean prescribed by law or regulation, often at the state level. For the first part of the question, the following were the results:

Prevalence of Standardized Tests

	No. of systems	Percent
Yes	108	61
No	69	39
Total	177	100

[No response 10]

Clearly, some of those who responded "no" meant that standardized tests were used, but by virtue of *state* mandating. This ambiguity should not substantially affect the answers to the second part of the question, to which multiple answers were possible:

How Are Test Results Used?

	No. of systems
Improve curriculum	41
Improve student performance	17
Placement/promotion/graduation requirements	16
School comparisons	14
Parents/public information	11
Teacher evaluation	4
Total	103

The answers to this question are one small piece of evidence bearing on an important current policy issue: should the results of standardized tests be used for internal or external judgment, for evaluation *within* a school (of its curriculum design, pedagogical practices, etc.) or *of* a school (and its "output"). The top-ranking three responses, together with the last (teacher evaluation), suggest the former. However, aiming test results at parents or the public may amount to providing a measure of how well an individual student is doing, where a class stands in relation to a national norm, or how "good" the school's scores are. This ambiguity, taken together with the fact that respondents from a relatively large number of systems (about 75) did not respond or responded confusingly, may indicate that the purposes of standardized testing are not well understood.

◆   CP8   How are textbooks selected?

Decision-Making on Textbook Choice

	No. of systems	Percent
Individual teachers	28	18
Social studies department (school)	28	18
Teachers recommend, district committee selects	12	8
District committee with teacher input	52	33
Districts teachers review, school administration selects	16	10
State review, district committee selects	24	15
Total	160	100
[No response 22]		

These results are generally consonant with those for questions CP6(a) and 6(b). The first two patterns represent local school-based decisions, the next two district-level negotiation (in either case, with strong teacher input). The latter set together account for 41 percent of the cases. The last set of two responses are opposites: in one case, teachers select those texts that are acceptable to them, and the school administrator then makes the final choice (limited by the teachers' slates); in the other, the state determines which texts meet its requirements, after which the district committee (including teachers) may choose. (In the latter case, some teachers will have been involved in the state committee's initial limiting of the field.)

◆   CP9   Please describe general staff development programs that are offered to social studies teachers by the school or the school district.

Although this question was contained in a questionnaire entitled *Curriculum Requirements/Organization*, some respondents interpreted "general staff development" to refer to pedagogy in a broad sense as well as content-specific pedagogy and the continuing education of teachers in content areas. An analysis of where such programs are initiated, or who takes responsibility for them, revealed the following:

	No. of systems	Percent
District develops programs	85	49
District/schools develop programs	25	15
Schools develop program	5	3
Programs externally initiated	13	8
Do not have programs	45	26
Total	173	100
	[No response 9]	

In general, such programs are conducted at the district level, with some variation across schools in the district. (Even externally initiated enrichment or in-service programs, begun by or with professional educational or disciplinary organizations, are generally put into place at the level of the district or districts.) Over one quarter of the systems seem to have no such programs at all.

◆   CP10   Please describe what you feel to be the strengths and weaknesses of your current social studies program.

The information obtained from this open-ended question is discussed in some detail in Section 5 of this report.

Teacher Characteristics and Opinions

◆ TP2 [Teacher Profile] How many years have you taught social studies?

Contrary to some impressionistic suggestions in the literature, that social studies teachers tend to be either relatively new or relatively longterm teachers, our A-R respondents show a fairly normal distribution. For all teachers, the data are as follows:

	Years Teaching Social Studies							
	0-3	3-5	6-10	11-15	16-20	21-25	26-30	31+
Percent of Teachers	9	5	18	19	23	14	8	4

In terms of their employment as elementary, middle school, or secondary teachers of social studies, the following figure shows little difference across grade levels.

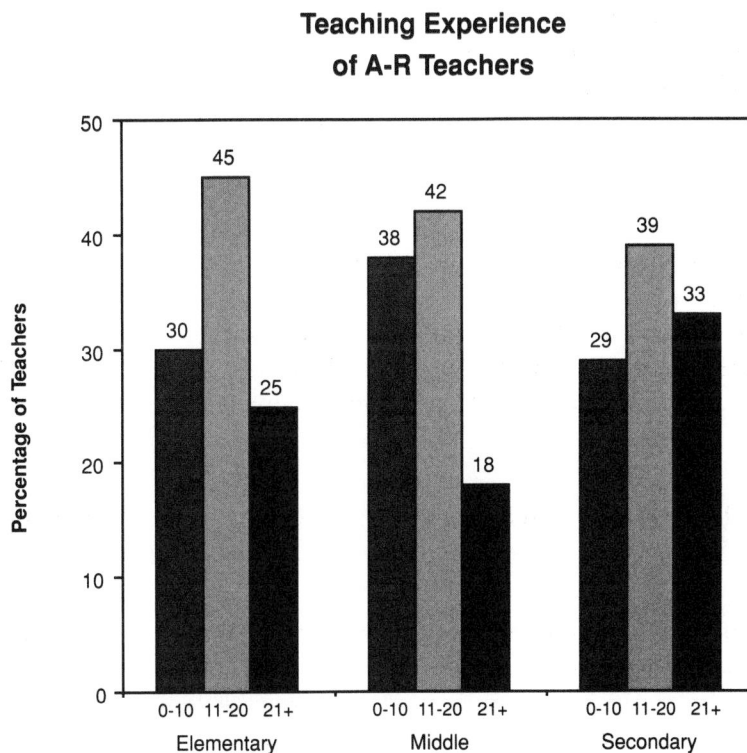

Teaching Experience of A-R Teachers

Figure 6

That relatively fewer middle school teachers have 20 or more years is at least partly due to the fact that "middle school" is still a fairly new institution in a number of systems.

◆   TP3   Number of periods per week you teach social studies; number
              of minutes per period (Cf CP3)

Since the length of instructional periods commonly varies across elementary, middle, and secondary school, the data here are reported as number of instructional hours per week in social studies. The grade levels along the horizontal axis are chosen so as to reflect the pattern of A-R respondents teaching social studies at a particular grade or across grades (thus, for example, more of our teachers teach social studies in grades 7 *and* 8 than in 7 alone or 8 alone).

Grades Where A-R Teachers Teach Social Studies *

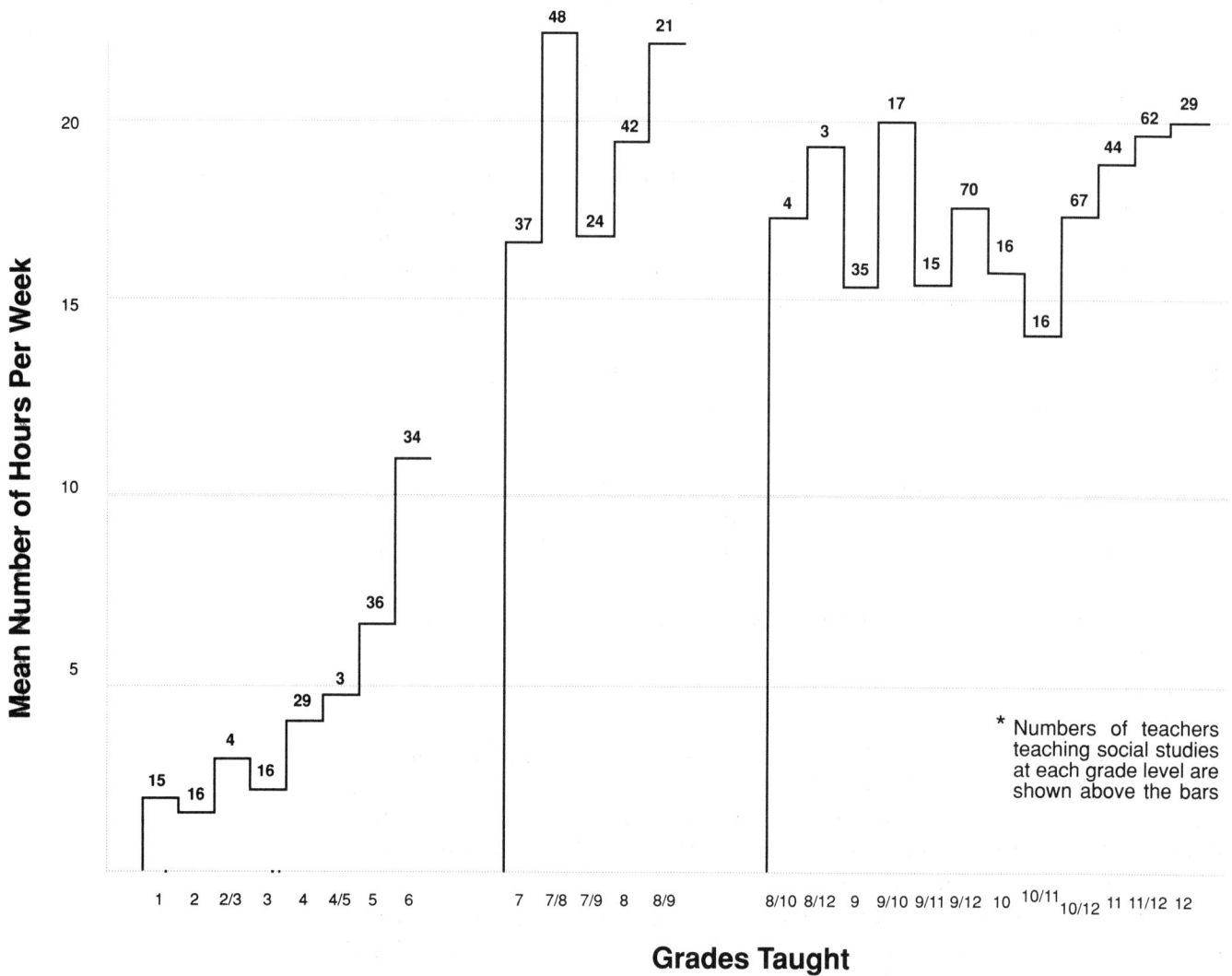

Figure 7

The results show that social studies instruction steps up sharply from 4-5 through 6; and that instruction localized to single grades is relatively less prevalent from grade 7 onward (than instruction given by these teachers across adjacent grades), with the exception of grade 12 (and possibly grade 11). Many curriculum studies have shown that in recent years little social studies is *required* in grades 9 and 10. The present data suggest that, in addition, relatively few social studies electives are available in the A-R schools.

In general, the most social studies instruction among A-R teachers takes place in grades 7 to 9 and 11 to 12. In some of these grades, A-R teachers report teaching 20 or more hours a week, which accounts for most of the instructional time (25 hours) per week reported as a national average for precollegiate teachers.[11]

Using combined grade-level categories, the weighted mean number[12] of social studies hours taught is:

Grades	1-3	4-6	7-10	9-12
Hours	1.9	7.0	19.6	17.3

Could the amount of social studies instruction conducted by the A-R teachers be related to competing *nonacademic* responsibilities, perhaps differently at different grade levels? For example, if upper elementary (grades 4-6) teachers have heavy duties in in-school monitoring, bus or lunchroom duty, or the like, it might explain their lower average social studies teaching workload.

◆   TP4   Do you have other school responsibilities? Number of hours per week for those assignments.

Those *with* non-teaching responsibilities at the grade levels were:

	Elementary	Middle	Secondary
Percent of teachers	40	77	86

Among those with such responsibilities, the ratios of *number of responsibilities* per teacher were:

Duties per teacher	.61	1.14	.99

Apparently, those with the *heaviest* social studies teaching loads—middle-school teachers, see TP3—also have the *heaviest* nonacademic duty load. Among secondary-level teachers, coaching accounted for 21% of the cited duties, followed closely by involvement with a special interest club (17%) or service on an internal school committee (15%).

We do not have data on to what extent teaching in other curriculum areas competes, at the various levels, with social studies. (For teachers' educational backgrounds, however, see TP8.)

◆   TP5   List titles or topics of social studies courses you currently teach.

Number of Mentions

	E	M	S	T
American History	29	119	183	331
AP American History	0	3	18	21
World History	12	26	63	101
AP World History	0	0	8	8
European History	0	3	16	19
Western Civilization	0	1	16	17
State/Local History	17	42	30	89
American Government	3	16	72	91
Civics	1	18	20	39
Political Science	1	3	9	13
Law	0	1	16	17
International Relations	0	0	7	7
All Subjects, including				
social studies	51	0	0	51
Expanding Horizons	46	0	0	46
"Social Studies"	0	13	16	29
Geography	26	60	29	115
Global Studies	0	5	19	24
Area Studies	0	5	18	23
Asian or African Studies	0	0	2	2
Anthropology	0	4	7	11
World Cultures	9	14	26	49
Economics	4	11	50	65
Consumer Education	0	0	2	2
Psychology	0	4	35	39
Sociology	0	4	23	27
American Studies	0	1	8	9
Humanities	0	0	6	6
Philosophy	0	0	4	4
Miscellaneous	0	8	41	49
No. of Titles/Topics	199	361	744	1304
No. Teachers Responding	150	211	371	732
[No. Teachers in Sample	175	223	379	777]

In this question, "titles or topics" presumably tends to dispose responses toward named major units of instruction. Considering the number of elementary teachers who responded All Subjects or Expanding Horizons, it is not surprising that the number of different distinct titles offered is lowest for them. This also implies that nearly all elementary teachers may teach considerable American History or Geography, even though those titles are not separately listed. Since some teachers who teach predominantly in grades 4 to 6 (as opposed to K to 3) may be classified in the M column, this may also suggest that there is more "titled" teaching in the elementary schools in our sample than appears here.

Relatedly, it does not appear—as some recent curriculum critics have charged—that "Expanding Horizons" or, especially, "Social Studies" dominates the curriculum, even at the elementary level. The related idea, that "Social Studies" drops entirely out of the curriculum in the higher grades, also is not borne out in these data.

That Civics is mentioned as many times in S as in M reflects the assignment of those teaching grade 9 in the sample. Note that Law is cited nearly as often as Civics in S. If all 9th-grade citations were removed from S here, no doubt Law would be far *more* frequently mentioned, relative to Civics. Law is also cited more frequently than Political Science.

Although Geography is strong at M, it is not entirely clear what content is emphasized in the other titles in this group. Probably a non-geographic disciplinary basis is evident in S, so that for example World Cultures there is different from World Cultures in E or M, which may be largely human geography.

"Free enterprise" economics is virtually absent in our responses. World History appears strongly at both M and S, relative to European History or Western Civilization.

◆   TP6   List titles or topics of social studies courses you have taught in the past seven years.

Number of Mentions

	Elementary	Middle	Secondary	Total
American History	28	135	222	385
AP American History	0	2	14	16
World History	10	49	81	140
AP World History	0	0	7	7
European History	1	4	21	26
Western Civilization	0	3	19	22
State/Local History	17	49	24	90
American Government	4	18	89	111
Civics	1	27	17	45
Political Science	0	7	5	12
Law	0	5	21	26
International Relations	0	0	5	5
All Subjects, including social studies	58	0	0	58
Expanding Horizons	40	0	0	40
"Social Studies"	0	16	22	38
Geography	20	58	61	139
Global Studies	1	3	21	25
Area Studies	2	9	18	29
Asian or African Studies	0	0	3	3
Anthropology	0	3	13	16
World Cultures	7	20	37	64
Economics	2	14	59	75
Consumer Education	0	0	0	0
Psychology	0	8	44	52
Sociology	0	7	41	48
American Studies	0	4	9	13
Humanities	0	0	4	4
Philosophy	0	0	1	1
Miscellaneous	0	5	46	51
No. of Titles or Topics	191	446	904	1541
No. of Teachers Responding	136	201	360	697
[No. Teachers in Sample	175	223	379	777]

Slightly fewer teachers responded to this question than to TP5, but the relative numbers of teachers from E, M, and S were about the same. Since a seven-year period was involved, it is not surprising that the total number of mentions of titles or topics was somewhat higher among teachers in M and S than in TP5.

Because, to a very great degree, the *same* teachers responded to TP6 as to TP5, because what these teachers are currently teaching is included in these data, and because more recent courses might be better remembered than ones taught several years previously, there is some inherent bias against the data for TP6 being radically different from those of TP5. Allowing for this, it is still remarkable how similar the two tables are. (Bear in mind that the actual *number* of mentions tend consistently to be greater in TP6.)

Comparing these two tables, there is some suggestion that State/Local History has become somewhat more common in S, and Civics less prevalent in M; that Geography has tended to shift over the past seven years from S to M; and that among electives Sociology may have lost ground in S. All of these possibilities are consistent with recent curriculum literature, but the present data cannot offer more than casual evidence. The prudent over-all conclusion would be that, in our sample of teachers, the social studies curriculum has undergone little change since the early 1980s.

Finally, with regard to courses taught, recall that CP4 reported data on the number of *elective* courses offered in the *systems* in which our A-R teachers work. When the heavily elective subjects from that question are compared to those same subjects in TP5, in terms of number of courses taught, it bears out a comment made in the discussion of TP5. When a subject is predominantly elective, the teachers in our study teach only a portion of the courses offered in their systems (e.g., Behavioral Science in CP4 accounted for 194 courses, whereas our teachers in TP5 teach only 76 courses of psychology, sociology, and anthropology). Obviously, the balance of such known courses are taught by teachers not enrolled in our study. (Some psychology teachers do not consider themselves social studies teachers at all.) By contrast, our teachers report teaching several hundred history courses and over a hundred government courses—a far greater number of courses in these areas than were listed as *electives*. Although there may be some indeterminacy about the number of *sections* involved in these numbers, clearly the main reason for this difference between the two listings is that our respondents to TP5 are citing courses that are heavily *required*.

◆   TP7   What is the average size of the social studies classes you teach?

The results for our respondents as a group are shown in Figure 8.

**Class Size
for A-R Teachers**

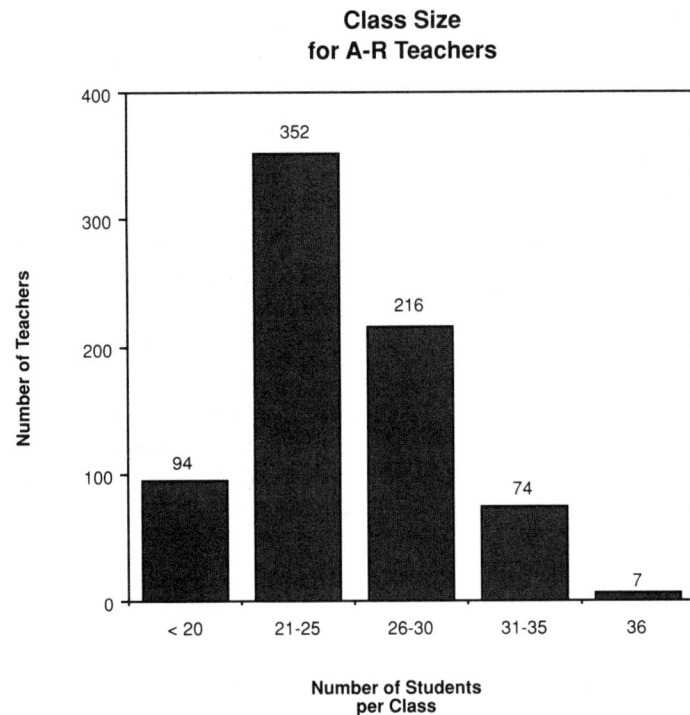

Figure 8

A break-down by Elementary, Middle, and Secondary shows that early elementary teachers tend to have class sizes at or below 25; upper elementary teachers, between 21 and 30. About as many middle school teachers have class sizes smaller than 20 *or* larger than 30 (their mean is about 25). Very few secondary classes are smaller than 20, whereas a substantial number are larger than 30. In brief, classes in the earlier grades tend to be small; in grades 10-12, there is a less marked tendency for them to be large.

◆   TP8   Educational Background

The (pre-service) educational background of our A-R teachers is interesting in itself, given recent controversy over "education" versus academic subject preparation and given some controversy within social studies over which are the most important subject areas. These data may also be important in the adequate specification of our study population, since it is conceivable that teachers' responses to some of the opinion and attitude items in the various questionnaires (as opposed to items asking for factual answers) might depend on their backgrounds.

We categorized teachers' stated backgrounds into three *levels*—bachelor's degrees, master's degrees, and post-master's degrees—and into six educational degree *fields*—education, specialized education, "social studies," history, other social science field, and non-social-science subject field. Initially we distinguished between those with degrees in general education and those with degrees in specialized aspects such as reading, bilingual education, school administration, learning disabilities, and the like. Since there were relatively few of the latter, specialized education was combined with "education" in our report. (In our study, it was relatively unlikely that a teacher not involved in classroom work in social studies would participate; hence those with specialized backgrounds would tend to be few.) As the quotation marks indicate, we separate those with *degrees* called "social studies" (some of whom may have substantial academic subject area preparation) from those with degrees in academic fields, on the assumption that pre-service education involved at least an exposure to the concept of a fused or multidisciplinary teaching arena rather than simply individual teaching fields. We distinguish between those with history preparation from those with majors (or the equivalent) in political science, geography, economics, and the other fields of the social sciences most closely related to precollegiate social studies teaching. Finally, some social studies teachers in our study have backgrounds in French, German, English, American Studies, mathematics, and the like.

For clarity of presentation, we show in two separate tables below the *proportion of all* teachers with bachelor's degrees (as the highest attained level, independent of in-service credits) at each teaching level by the area of educational preparation, and the corresponding data for those with master's degrees. We then combine these two.[13]

Bachelor's Degrees

	% of total			sum of %s	rank
	E	M	S		
Education	17	12	5	34	1
Social Studies	1	8	14	23	3
History	1	5	21	27	2
Other SS field	-	2	5	7	5
Non-SS field	3	2	4	9	4
				100	

Master's Degrees

	% of total			sum of %s	rank
	E	M	S		
Education	16	17	21	54	1
Social Studies	1	2	9	12	3
History	1	4	16	21	2
Other SS field	1	2	6	9	4
Non-SS field	1	-	3	4	5
				100	

Combined Bachelor's and Master's Degrees

	% of total			sum of %s	rank
	E	M	S		
Education	16	14	12	42	1
Social Studies	1	6	12	19	3
History	1	5	19	25	2
Other SS field	-	2	5	7	4
Non-SS field	2	1	2	5	5
				100	

At each level and in the combined distribution, the rank orders of educational background are essentially the same. At the bachelor's level, more of our elementary teachers had majored in fields *other than* a social studies field, which affected the row %s and ranks. Otherwise, our teachers *generally* have backgrounds in Education, History, "Social Studies," another social science, and a non-social-science/studies academic field, in that order.

Degrees in Education were *relatively* more prevalent at both E and S than at M. This may reflect contingencies of professional advancement, together with the fact that M teachers tend to be younger than E or S (e.g., the perceived importance of Education degrees may have diminished somewhat in their pre-service cohort). Interestingly, the "Social Studies" degree was prevalent among both M and S teachers. (Some recent critics have held that a "social studies" background was a problem for the field especially at the elementary level.)

By far the most common *field* degree at all teaching levels is History. That background is the most common one, other than general education, at both educational attainment levels and at all teaching levels. It is relatively *more* prominent among those with bachelor's degrees than those with master's degrees. Not surprisingly, backgrounds in *other* social sciences are more common among Secondary teachers, but not by a lot proportionally. We infer that many social science elective courses in secondary school (see CP 4, TP6) are taught by teachers with History or Social Studies backgrounds. Among those in our study who report degrees in the social sciences other than History, the only fairly frequent field is political science/government.

◆　TP10　To what degree do you feel you have freedom to plan lessons, select materials and methods? (Very little? A moderate degree? A great deal?)

◆　TP11　To what degree do you feel comfortable in dealing with controversial issues in the classroom? (Idem)

◆　TP12　Currently, many critics of education claim that values are not being taught in the classrooms. To what degree do you feel you are teaching values? (Idem)

In the questionnaire, these three items were placed as a unit on the page, and, as expected, tended to be answered in a three-part format or with obvious interdependency across answers. This aspect of format and sequence may partly account for the fact that teachers as a group tended to give the same pattern of response to all three questions.

**Teachers' Reports
of Autonomy in the Classroom**

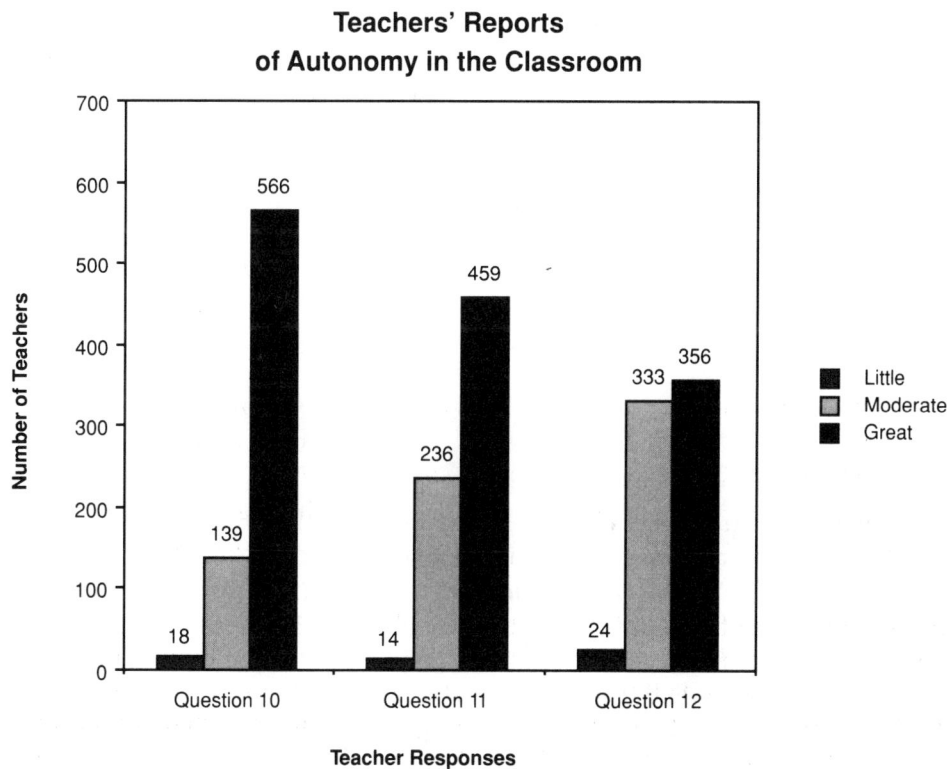

Figure 9

That teachers were more nearly split on the matter of whether or not they were teaching values than on their professional freedom to conduct classes and deal with controversial issues does not necessarily mean that the respondents did not consider and respond to all three questions together, to some degree.

That is, the fact that the overwhelming majority of teachers feel autonomous in planning lessons, choosing materials, etc., could in many individual cases *depend* on the teacher's accepting only a moderate degree of freedom in dealing with issues and on *not* feeling obliged to teach values very overtly or explicitly. Many other such dependencies are possible: e.g., that those who feel comfortable about teaching values feel well supported by the school administration and the community, so that freedom in choosing materials, planning lessons, etc., is a nonissue; etc.

In qualitative analysis of the written comments, we noted, most strikingly, that extended comments on the role of values were much more numerous and lengthier than on the other two matters. For TP10, most of the few additional comments that were written on the form were some version of "Freedom, but no time."

There is a probably important difference between E, M, and S-level teachers in one, possibly two, of these questions, as shown below.

		Percent responding:		
Level	No response	Very little	Moderate degree	Great degree
◆ TP10	*plan lessons*			
E	10	3	21	69
M	1	2	23	74
S	2	2	15	81
◆ TP11	*deal with issues*			
E	10	2	40	48
M	4	2	39	57
S	6	2	24	76
◆ TP12	*teaching values*			
E	3	2	36	59
M	2	4	48	46
S	4	3	47	46

Except for the high level of No Response to TP10 and TP11 among E teachers, the pattern of responses is very similar across teaching level. (S teachers feel particularly comfortable in dealing with controversial issues, in part as a function of the more advanced age and developmental level of their students.) With regard to teaching values, however, both M and S teachers split more or less evenly; only E teachers are strongly in the teaching-values profile. Whether or not values *are* and *should be* taught is clearly the most contentious area.

Inspecting the responses distributively, we find no immediately obvious differences that can be attributed to length of service (TP2), geographical area, type of school, or type of community (CP2, 3, 6), but a more powerful analysis might reveal such differences.

The proportions of respondents who wrote additional comments to TP12 were:

E: 51%   M: 30%   S: 37%

The bulk of those commenting were those who felt they did teach values either implicitly or explicitly. Elementary teachers stressed good citizenship and proper behavior. Middle school and secondary teachers were more apt to mention the interrelationship of values with the content they were covering—American history, government, world history, and world cultures.

About a fourth of the teachers commenting said something like, "Of course, the real issue is not whether we teach values, but rather what values do we teach?" Only those in denominational schools spoke of religious values. Perhaps a tenth of the respondents indicated a hostile climate to the teaching of values. Some mentioned the administration as wary of the practice; others suggested the school board and some parents made it difficult. Most seemed to feel that the values of citizenship and "social" values were safe and felt they were doing a good job of transmitting appropriate values in those areas.

Further research on the place of teaching values is likely to be important. A single question such as TP12, even permitting additional comments, will not suffice.

◆   TP13a   To what degree do you coordinate instruction with other social studies teachers in your school? (Very little? Moderate degree? Great degree?)

◆   TP13b   To what degree do you coordinate instruction with other social studies teachers in your school district? (idem)

◆   TP14   To what degree do you coordinate your instruction with that of other disciplines in your school? For example, Language Arts, Science, Music, Art? (idem)

The same teachers tended to respond to these three questions, both in terms of checking off the short answer (degree to which the statement was true) and in terms of supplying written comments. Perhaps partly (but not entirely) for this reason, about the same number of responses were received from each teaching level for the three questions (e.g., the same number of E teachers for each question), and the distribution of Very Little, Moderate Degree, Great Degree was essentially the same *within the three teaching levels* for TP13a and 13b.

Every day children bring issues to the classroom to be discussed. (E - Massachusetts)

One cannot teach American government without teaching the values of this nations political-economic system. One cannot compare systems without comparing values. (S - California)

The entire teaching of history is transmission of the everchanging value system. (S - Wisconsin)

Number of Teachers Responding:

		No Response	Very Little	Moderate Degree	Great Degree
◆	TP13a	*coordinate with social studies in school*			
		21	160	370	193
◆	TP13b	*coordinate with social studies in district*			
		52	329	259	95
◆	TP14	*coordinate with other disciplines*			
		19	358	271	97

Clearly, within-school coordination for social studies is more prevalent than within-district coordination for social studies or within-school coordination with other departments. Written comments explaining the lack of district coordination cited logistics and administrative attitudes: "The heavy schedule we all carry does not allow meetings outside the school"; "Our district is too big...to get together"; and "Our district actively discourages coordination across the system."

For TP14, the M and S teachers showed about the same pattern (much like the over-all pattern shown above for the group as a whole), but E teachers responded Moderate or Great somewhat more often. We suspect that there is a difference in expectations about cross-disciplinary cooperation. Elementary teachers supplying written comments frequently mentioned that they as individuals taught many or nearly all subjects, and that their "content" work was routinely coordinated with music and art and even physical education. It is likely that E teachers used a higher implicit standard for what "coordination" would mean than M or S teachers, and even so are reporting what is actually the case—that there is more cross-subject cooperation.

Those M teachers who commented on this kind of coordination mentioned the Writing Across the Curriculum program as being a spur toward more consistent coordination. Several mentioned problems: lack of time, turnover in teaching staff, resistance from colleagues; most of those did cite the advantages for the students and the desire on their own part to do more coordinated, interdisciplinary work. In the recent literature, there has been considerable interest in the "middle school" curriculum as a special opportunity for using multidisciplinary and "fused" subject matter content. The reasoning is that by the middle grades students have mastered the basic skills in various broad content areas, but are not yet ready for in-depth instruction in the particular methodologies of disciplines, which is thought to be more appropriate for high school. Such goals, approaches, and reasoning are not especially prominent among the middle school teachers in the A-R network, although there is nothing that would argue against them.

Secondary teachers more consistently mentioned specific programs that they were involved in, such as American Studies, Humanities, and Writing Lab as successful programs. They too were concerned with lack of time and with uninterested colleagues. Several stressed the benefits of team teaching and the importance of scheduling that fostered cross disciplinary work. Twelve teachers mentioned their frustration that time and scheduling problems could not be overcome, even when they themselves were eager to do more.

◆   TP15   If you can divide your teaching emphasis, what approximate percentages of classroom instruction do you spend on content learning and on skills development?

In teacher education, pedagogy research, and educational policy discussion much attention has been given over the past 30 years or more to the question of content *versus* skills. Thus many or most of the respondents will have interpreted the question as involving something approximating a forced choice, and a possibly crucial forced choice at that. A relatively high proportion of those in the sample answered this question with usable responses (624 out of 777), but it is possible that the 150 or so who did not respond chose not to because they did not accept a forced-choice premise.

In an established either/or situation, where there are strong advocates for both positions, there might be a strong bias toward the modal response being 50:50. Although few if any recommend a total emphasis on content or on skills, in an era of demand for h igher achievement and 'excellence' in the curriculum, a significant number of those involved with this issue have been promoting a redressing of the balance toward *more* content and *less* skills emphasis in instruction. Hardly anyone has promoted the complement of this. Thus it might be reasonable, *a priori*, to predict that a group of teachers drawn nationally would endorse some form of balance between the two together with a *relative* emphasis on content, these two response tendencies representing two tendencies, with different weights, in the *same* teachers or two *subgroups* of teachers. The latter would appear to be evident in the response from our sample as a whole. The four responses that range from 80:20 toward content over skills to 50:50 for content and skills make up the large majority of responses.

Content vs Skills in Instructional Emphasis

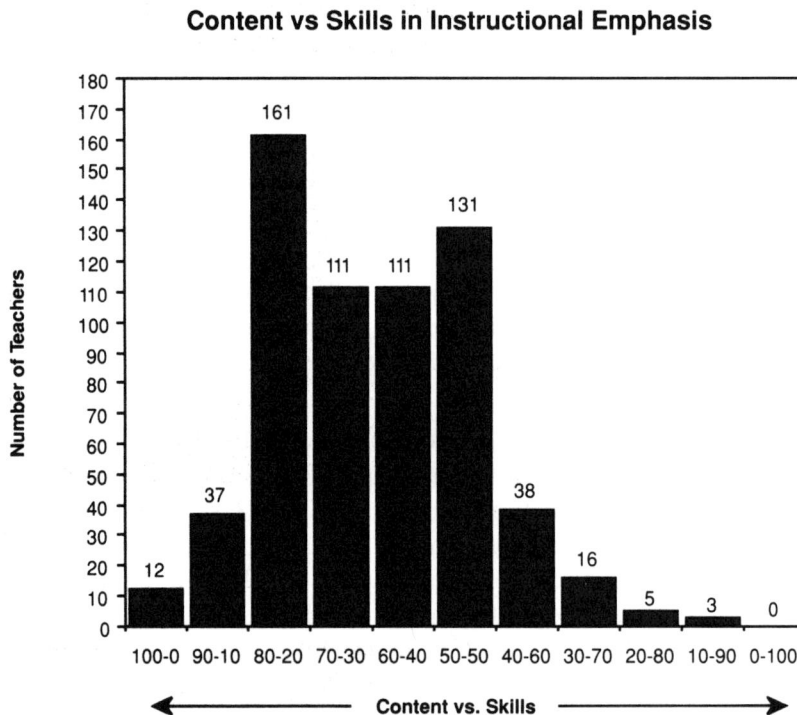

Figure 10

The discussion changes somewhat, however, and teacher opinions may change, as a function of grade level of instruction. Generally speaking, "basic skills" have been thought to be specially crucial for elementary instruction; discipline-based content has been assumed to be relatively more feasible at the secondary level. The matter is not simple: in recent pedagogical debates, for example, much attention has been given to the promotion of basic skills *through* subject content in E, and methodological skill *in* a particular content domain in S.

In analyzing nonresponders to this question, the percentage of teachers at each level who did not answer (in a usable form) were

     E: 39%   M: 11%   S: 18%

This may mean that teachers in E found the question difficult or that they experienced some strain between their (supposed) tendency as a group to believe skills development very important in the early grades and the tone of recent discussion, urging that content be increased in those grades.

When teacher respondents are segregated by E, M, and S, clearcut differences emerge.

I have to say that I emphasize concept learning and greater critical thinking. Sometimes I feel remiss that my students may not get as much content as others. I also spend a great deal of time on skill-research recording, map/graph/chart reading and interpretation. (E - Indiana)

**Emphasis on Content vs Skills
by Educational Level**

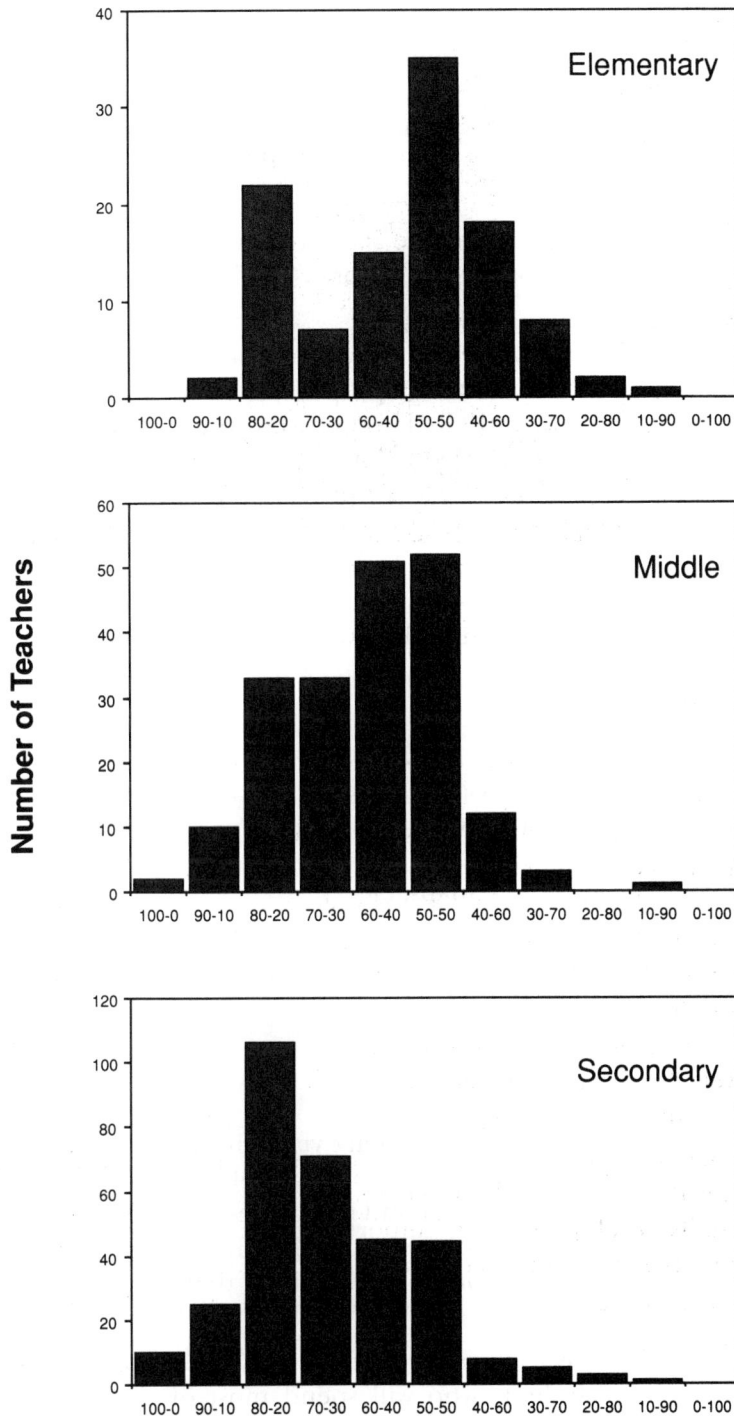

Difficult to separate. Skills are always taught within content! (M - Colorado)

Varies with lessons and issues. (S - New York)

Figure 11

In E and M, there is a central tendency to respond 50:50 or 60:40, and *beyond this* to emphasize content somewhat more than the skills dimension. That tendency is more clearcut among M teachers. Among S teachers, the sum of 50:50 and 60:40 is considerable, but responses to the set of content-over-skills options are even stronger. Thus, the distribution of responses for the group as a whole is heavily influenced by the S pattern, owing to the numbers involved. In general, M teachers seem most balanced, as a group, which is hardly surprising, since in the middle grades content and skills are generally meant to be closely interrelated. Unless the high nonresponse rate of E teachers is taken as an interfering factor, there is little evidence that E teachers are *strongly* oriented toward skills instruction in a way that would correspond to the definite orientation among S teachers toward content.

◆   TP17   Please list and rate instructional materials (other than textbooks) you frequently use. (Cf CP10)

Because students find textbooks boring and my biggest problem is getting them to read assignments, I pick and choose from the text and supplement it with primary source materials, articles, etc. (S - Virginia)

About 500 different teachers responded to this question: the number of E, M, and S responders were in rough proportion to the presence of E, M, and S teachers in the study as a whole. However, E teachers cited an average of 2.4 *types* of materials (as categorized below) per response; M teachers, 2.1; and S teachers, 1.8. Evidently, and not surprisingly, E teachers depend most on materials other than texts.

When the cited materials are classified into different types, they rank in frequency of citation as follows, with the *over-all* rank shown (from most to least) in the order of the listing and ranks given separately for each teaching level.[14]

Type	E	M	S
Media—video, movies, etc.	2	1**	1
Supplementary printed—books, etc.	1	1**	2
Newspapers, magazines, etc.	5	3	3
Geographic aids—globes, maps, etc.	3	4	4
Local resources—speakers, self-made exhibits, etc.	4	5	5
Computer software	6	6	6
Simulations—games, kits, etc.	7	7	7
** tied rank			

The series we are using now is one of the best I have ever used. It meets almost all our learning outcomes. (E - West Virginia)

The rankings for M and S teachers are virtually identical. The ranking for E teachers is very similar in most categories, except that E teachers use the visual media a little less, and newspaper and magazines markedly less, than teachers at other levels. This presumably indicates that there are more supplementary books available at the appropriate reading level than there are periodicals.

◆   TP18   What is your vision of effective, useful social studies instruction for students who will spend most of their lives in the 21st century? If you could wave a magic wand, what would you wish the social studies program to be?

For discussion of information gained from this open-ended question, see Section 5 of this Report.

4. Further Attitudes and Opinions: Questionnaires A and B

Some months after the Community Profile and the Teacher Profile produced information about the nature of social studies in some of the nation's systems, and about the characteristics and background and problems of teachers of social studies, two additional questionnaires, focussing on teacher attitudes, opinions, preferences, and intentions, were administered through the Adviser-Responder School Network.

Fewer teachers in the study population completed these latter two questionnaires than had completed the Teacher Profile.[15] It is not known to what extent this reflects a lessening of interest in the project or the fact that Questionnaires A and B called for longer, more thoughtful, and more judgmental responses.

Characteristics of the Later Sample

The number of teachers participating in the various phases of the study are as follows.

Numbers of Teachers

	Elementary	Middle	Secondary	Total
Teacher Profile	175	223	379	777
Questionnaire A	43	88	144	275
Questionnaire B	35	75	137	247
[Responding to both	27	49	114	190]

Percent at Teaching Level

	Elementary	Middle	Secondary
Teacher Profile	22.5	28.7	48.7
Questionnaire A	15.6	32.0	52.4
Questionnaire B	14.1	30.4	55.5

Although the number of teachers responding dropped off sharply for Questionnaires A and B, eventually producing low numbers especially at the elementary level, virtually all of those answering the later questionnaires were the same persons who had participated in the study to that date. Some individual teachers skipped A and completed B; some, vice versa. We can feel confident that those responding to the two later questionnaires were well informed about the study and that, having participated earlier, they gave reliable and probably "richer" data than would teachers confronted only with these questionnaires.

As the table above indicates, the proportion of elementary teachers declined from questionnaire to questionnaire more rapidly than for the two other levels. Part of this decline is attributable to the nature of the questions, some of which were not very relevant to elementary teaching.

However, the question arises: did the general decline in respondents alter the fundamental or background characteristics of the study population? If this were so, the data summaries of school systems and teachers in the preceding part of this chapter, although interesting as descriptions of *a* self-selected American "social studies universe," might not apply well to this later, smaller, even more highly self-selected, group.

In the comparisons that follow, we combine data from those who responded to questionnaires A and B (without double-counting those who responded to both).

	Percents			
regional distribution	East	Central	Mountain	Pacific
CP	46	33	8	11
A-B	60	25	8	6

type of system	Urban	Suburban	Rural/Town
CP	36	38	25
A-B	31	44	25

socio-economic status of system	Affluent	Mid.Class	Low.Class	Mixed
CP	12	30	19	39
A-B	21	40	8	30

time teaching (years)	0-10	11-20	21+
CP	32	42	26
A-B	25	43	32

Those who responded to A and B were somewhat more Eastern, and from relatively more middle- to upper-SES systems. When these characteristics were broken down by level of teaching—E, M, and S—the secondary teachers responding to A and B were more like the S teachers of the entire study population than was true of E and M teachers. This is probably a statistical effect; the S group was the largest of the three, and thus in terms of statistical characteristics would be the most stable, other things equal.

The area of educational preparation for the teachers participating in A and B is as follows (compare TP8).*

	Percents			% Sums	Rank
	E	M	S		
Education	9	9	3	21	3
Social Studies	1	10	20	31	2
History	1	8	29	38	1
Other SS Field	-	3	4	7	4
Non-SS Field	-	1	1	2	5

* Here we tally the highest *teaching-relevant* degree (i.e., excluding advanced degrees in educational administration and the like).

Although we do not believe that we are dealing, in A and B, with a different "universe" of social studies, the regional and SES differences should be kept in mind in what follows. The most obvious discrepancy involves the area of educational background of the teachers responding to A and B. Especially among M and S teachers, their backgrounds are much less likely to have been in Education, and more likely to have been in History or Social Studies *per se*. (The latter is true especially of S teachers.) That *both* History and Social Studies are much more strongly represented in the A-B study population than in the over-all population implies that, to the extent that A-B questions deal with possible tensions or choices *between* History and Social Studies, this issue might be sharply drawn—assuming that a teacher's educational background makes a difference in that teacher's opinions and preferences.

Questionnaire A: Curriculum Design and Emphasis

The most general and comprehensive question put to the Questionnaire A teachers is given in A7, below. Readers may want to examine that item first. On the other hand, most respondents will have answered the question after answering the ones directly following.

◆   A2   How should history and the social sciences be related within the curriculum?

Gist of Response	% generating response
History as the core; social sciences connected or supplemental to history; history alone	53.4
History and social sciences closely related; interwoven, integrated; equally prominent	21.9
Relate past to present	6.1
Integrate both history and social science material with English, arts, science, etc.	5.3
Keep social sciences (other than history) separate	3.2

History should be the foundation discipline within social studies education. Teachers can draw upon other social sciences for supplementary content. (M - Nebraska)

I don't think we have the time to study any one discipline as a unit of specialized information. People cannot be fragmented into parts. The topic of social studies must be recognized as one where the whole is greater than its parts. (E - Illinois)

Relate the 'now' to the 'past.' The idea of relating what we are and how we got to where we are, had to have some beginning. (S - DoDDS Germany)

The first wording combines responses that gave History as the core *or*—for practical purposes—the sole subject matter, and that clearly saw other social science subjects as ancillary. The polar opposite response type would be to keep history and the social sciences separate: here, some respondents emphasized that geography needed separate exposition. The second and third types of response can be seen as similar. Those who dwelt on relating the past to the present typically specified the need for attention to contemporary economics, politics, social problems, etc., and to the historical background of these topics or dimensions. Although this is a somewhat different approach from that tracing, for example, economic or technological history, or the development over time of a political system and culture, the two approaches seemed complementary; both go well beyond using ahistorical social science concepts only to illuminate some special topics or eras in history.

If this interpretation is valid, then some 28 percent are in favor of a balanced, integrated history/social sciences curriculum. A 53%/28% balance seemingly in favor of the pre-eminence of history in the curriculum is *greater* than what one would predict if one were to assume that teachers' educational background would tend to determine their preferences (see above, p. 39). Among our respondents, there seems to be no danger of history's being downgraded or underemphasized.[16]

While they should be taught as separate disciplines, both should be used to strengthen knowledge about today's world, encourage the development of good decision-making skills, and foster the growth of a global view toward modern problems and issues. (S - Missouri)

It is relevant that those who favored keeping history and the other social sciences separate and those who favored a thorough integration of the two as equal partners came primarily from among S (and to a lesser extent, M) teachers. By contrast, those who favored a primacy for history were quite evenly spread over teaching levels (around 50% for each of the three levels). Those who favored an integration of history *and* other social studies *with* language arts, etc., were heavily M teachers. Probably, in this question, we have a mixture, in our results, of personal preferences or principles with a mirroring of present practice. That is (for example), separate courses are in fact taught in secondary, not elementary, schools; and it is middle school where cross-departmental arrangements most often occur.

History and literature are a natural relationship. I also see a relationship between history and foreign language and the arts—especially art history. (S - California)

◆   A3   Are some social sciences more important than others in developing a social studies curriculum? If so, which are these?

Response	% generating response
History	44.8
Equal importance; subject integration	17.2
Geography	12.3
Human society, behavioral sciences, global	10.0
Other social science (polit. sci., econ., et al.)	5.0

Despite the fact that the wording of the question (given A2, preceding) might seem to act against a strong response for history —"social sciences" could exclude history[17]—the fact that history was by far the most commonly specified is another indication of its secure role in the curriculum.

However, the question, by probing for *specific* subject names (unlike A2, which tended to oppose history to "the social sciences" as a group), tends to imply *essential* subject matter. Thus, some responses might reflect the teaching level, since it is commonly thought that some subjects are most crucial at certain grade levels. There is some evidence for the latter hypothesis, if we look at the percent *of each teaching level* who give particular importance to a given subject.

	% selecting at each level				
	Hist.	Geog.	Econ./ Govt.	Anthro./ Soc./Global	Equal
E	23.7	18.4	2.6	23.7	26.3
M	42.4	12.9	2.4	9.4	18.8
S	52.9	9.6	6.6	8.1	14.0

Since we established above that history is desired for the core of the curriculum by teachers of all three levels, and that anthropological/sociological/global and geographical material is seen as less *central*, the explanation for (for example) the fact that elementary-level teachers find anthro/soc/global as "important" as history, and geography nearly so, must have to do with the question of *when* it is *essential* to teach particular subjects. Thus, a number of elementary teachers may well teach much history, but still assume that history will be *mastered* at higher levels—and M and S teachers may agree with them. By contrast, geography and anthropological/sociological topics are particularly important *at* this level (and *in* the middle grades). Only an explanation like this would account for the relative paucity of selections of elective subjects at S, or the general nonselection of economics and government. As other data suggest (see A7), it is not that economics and government are not considered important, but that they are not viewed as crucial at certain grades. Similarly, that topics concerning other cultures and societies do not show up strongly at high school in this table may not mean that many or most secondary teachers do not agree with the idea that the social studies curriculum needs to be more nonparochial and globally oriented. but that that goal is not captured by giving a particular courses or courses pride of place in the curriculum. (Cf A7, A9)

The subject matter that is identifiable with one or another of the social sciences becomes includable in the curriculum to the extent that it provides interest and power in the history curriculum. (S - Oregon)

A well-rounded curriculum would combine them all. They are all important and interrelated, i.e., sociology-lifestyles and culture; psychology-how and why man thinks and behaves; history— events that have taken place from past to present. (M - Indiana)

◆   A6   What do you consider to be the main purpose of social studies
                in the schools?

The over-all frequencies of response are as follows:

Response	% generating response
Developing skills for well-informed citizens (critical thinking, decision-making, etc., in amplification of factual knowledge)	55.2
Educated American citizenry; history, government, and economic systems; role as citizens; relation of past to present	12.1
American patriotism, values, role models	7.3
Global perspective, world interdependence	5.2
Relationship to broad environment (family, community; self and society; humanity)	4.8

The question itself is differently oriented from a content-oriented question, and produced a distinctly different distribution of responses (from that, for example, of A3 or A7). In public education generally, most broad curriculum areas draw legitimacy from the *main purpose* of producing well-informed citizens in a democratic society. The two leading response categories both reflect this overriding goal: the first gives emphasis to pragmatic knowledge in a society built on democratic participation, whereas the second emphasizes knowledge specially pertinent to this democratic society. The third response—American patriotism, etc.—may be seen as an extreme form of the second, perhaps dwelling more on allegiance than broad knowledge. A crude summary would call the first response Citizenship, the second and third together, Americanism. Judging by supplementary comments in the questionnaire responses, the strong emphasis on history *as content* apparent in A2, A3, and A7 is somewhat present in the Americanism responses, but not in the sense that history is the exclusive avenue toward the desired purpose: other subject matter—government, economics, etc.—is also mentioned toward this end. Similarly, citizenship skill is not based on simply knowledge of government forms and processes, or economic decision-making, or interpersonal relations. Nor are we dealing with a simple Skills vs. Content distinction: in the written answers in both of the leading response categories, both are cited.

What some education scholars have called the *pre-emptive* purpose of schooling—effective participation in society in the chosen mode of that society—probably appears in these results. On a subsidiary level, the written answers suggest that the Developing Skills response category is more or less neutral with regard to the relative importance of domestic versus transnational or global knowledge; both types are needed for well-informed citizens. The Educated American Citizenry response (12.1%) tends to emphasize domestic topics; *together*, the Global Perspective and Broad Environment responses (10.0%) are almost as common. Once again, there are marked differences by teaching level.

The main purpose is to teach students how to live in a democracy—to become informed, involved citizens who know, appreciate, and use what they learn to become active citizens—to learn to think critically, to question, and to make wise decisions. (M - Missouri)

To teach adequate education in the fundamental documents and principles upon which our freedoms evolved. A greater capacity to understand where we came from, where we are at, and where we are going as a nation. (M - Kansas)

	% selecting response[*]			
	Citizen-ship skills	American knowledge	Patriot-ism	Global/Envir. Perspective
Entire group	55.2	12.1	7.3	10.0
Elementary	48.7	15.4	2.6	12.9
Middle	50.6	10.1	6.3	12.6
Secondary	59.1	12.6	9.4	7.8

[*] As in the table above, percents do not add to 100; various "other" and noncodable responses are not reported.

Although all teaching levels select Citizenship Skills and American Knowledge about equally, some S teachers show a marked commitment to the strong form of Americanism and less of a commitment to global and intercultural/human environmental matters. E teachers reverse this pattern; M teachers fall between. A further analysis of the groups shows that E teachers have a strong commitment to *human relations* content and approaches—i.e., the interpersonal and universal or panhuman aspects—although M teachers are more focussed on global interdependency and cultural diversity.

◆ A7 What content do you believe is essential to achieving the purpose of social studies education?…for (a) primary and secondary, (b) middle school, (c) secondary

The number of teachers responding were:
E: 40   M: 78   S: 133

Teachers at all levels cited content essential to *all* school levels; there was no limit on the number of responses that could be given.

Number of Content Mentions[18]

		For each school level			
		E	M	S	Total
From	E	97	69	64	230
each	M	151	176	184	511
school	S	223	249	332	804
level	T	471	494	580	1545

To teach students that there are many cultures and subcultures within our nation and world. Give them enough knowledge to facilitate respect for others. Teach world interdependence, geography of the world, a basic understanding of global economics. (E - Arkansas)

Elementary teachers gave more content citations for elementary school than for other levels; secondary teachers, for secondary level. In general, however, teachers responded for each of the levels. (That is, although three times as many secondary level teachers in the sample as elementary teachers, there were only 22 percent more content mentions for the secondary level.)

In the table below, the numbers of content citations are ranked by essential content area, for the sample as a whole.

Number and Rank of Content Mentions

Rank	Content Area	No. of Mentions	*for* E	*for* M	*for* S	*from* E	*from* M	*from* S
1	History	441	114	147	180	59	165	217
2	Geography	286	101	129	56	31	102	153
3	Other*	253	129	60	64	63	65	125
4	Govt/Law/Civics	214	38	56	120	28	75	111
5	Global/Cross-Cult.	180	61	55	64	24	54	102
6	Economics	95	5	25	65	8	29	58
7	Behavioral**	76	23	22	31	17	21	38

* Other = Content-relevant skills; content inter-relationships; current issues
** Coding of mentions of psychology, sociology, and anthropology

By looking down the columns *for* Elementary, Middle, and Secondary, the content most recommended for these grade levels (by all teachers) is evident. By looking down the columns *from* Elementary, Middle, and Secondary, the source of these recommendations is given, in terms of the teaching levels of the teachers. The obvious concern, of course, is: do certain content recommendations come from certain teaching levels? For example, an extreme case would be that all recommendations for Geography as essential content, no matter for what level, would emanate from middle school teachers, while all recommendations for Economics would come from secondary teachers. The table reassures us that such is not the case.

For example, while there are only 5 citations of Economics *for* elementary school, 8 elementary level teachers recommend Economics as essential somewhere in the curriculum. With regard to rank 3, Other, inspection of the responses shows that teachers *from* E and M recommend emphasis on content interrelationships *for* E (and to a lesser extent, M), while teachers *from* S have critical thinking, decision-making, and attention to current issues primarily in mind when recommending Other *for* S.

The difference between rank 2, Geography, and rank 5, Global/Cross-Cultural, is instructive to analyze. While Geography as "essential" for E and M is no surprise, M and S teachers recommend this on a greater-than-one-for-one basis (owing to multiple mentions). Global/Cross-Cultural content is recommended *from* E, M, and S in proportion to the numbers of respondents from E, M, and S, but these recommendations are spread about equally *for* the three levels. It may be concluded, tentatively, that teachers in general value Geography *especially* at certain levels, while teachers who value Global/Cross-Cultural content do so at all levels. (Cf. A3)

The statistical complexities of dealing with teachers unequally drawn from the three levels but free to mention content any number of times for different levels makes further quantitative analysis suspect. For example, to weight a mention of History *for* the Middle School *from* an elementary teacher, by some factor reflecting the proportion of teachers at each level recommending History content or Middle School content, would involve assumptions about teacher representativeness or curriculum thinking that are uncalled for.

Based on the data presented thus far, we see little evidence for particular interactions that would distort the interpretation of the answers to the question. There are few recommendations that can be said to be localized to only one school level, or from only one level. For example, although most observers find that global and cross-cultural material and emphasis is particularly prevalent in middle school instruction, we find no special concentration toward this content in the middle school in these data. (These data, however, reflect the opinions of our teachers about what *ought* to be, and do not necessarily reflect what is actually taught in their own courses.)

A largely nonquantitative way of looking further for "pockets" of opinion as to essential content is offered in the table below, where rank-orders of content are shown, most preferred downward, *for* each school level as obtained *from* each school level. This presentation tends to minimize the effect of the unequal number of teachers from E, M, and S in generating recommendations for content.

Most-Recommended Content*

		for school level		
		E	M	S
	E	Other	History	History
		History	Other	Govt
		Geography	Geography	Other
		Global	Global	Geography=
		Govt	Govt	Economics
from school level	M	History	History	History
		Geography	Geography	Govt
		Other	Govt	Global
		Govt	Global	Economics
		Global	Other	Geography=
				Other
	S	Other	Geography	History
		History	History	Govt
		Geography	Govt=	Other
		Global	Global	Other
		Govt	Other	Geography=
				Global

* See preceding table for finer content detail. An equality sign indicates an approximate tie in rank order.

In summary, we see an impressive degree of over-all *concordance* in teachers' recommendations from and for the different levels. There is considerable evidence here that teachers, in recommending what is "essential," take into account the nature of elementary, middle, and secondary schools and the character of different subject matters in a relatively consensual fashion. Though it is impossible to know how much of the prevalent endorsement of History reflects the strong history backgrounds of this study group, there is no evidence for a nothing-but-history attitude in the group as a whole. In general, we do not see groups or types of teachers pushing "the middle school view" or "the geographical cause" or other favorite recipes. This will be reassuring in considering our teachers' opinions on other issues in this study.

◆   A4   What is the importance of the humanities (arts, literature, history, language, philosophy) in social studies education?

The inclusion of the term "history" in the specification of "the humanities" caused obvious confusion among some of the 246 respondents to this question. A sizeable number of those giving the most common response (see below) may have interpreted the question as, What is the importance of *history*, and an additional 7.7% focussed on history as a central element of the entire school curriculum, suggesting that both the humanities and the social studies could be incorporated into or interrelated by History.

Type of Response	% generating response
Essential: humanities bring insight, perspective, personal enrichment	55.7
Humanities are of equal importance with social studies; they should be integrated	20.7
History is the over-all bridge or framework	7.7
Humanities provide examples, should be infused into social studies	4.5

The most frequent response was given by teachers from all three levels, about proportionately. The second most frequent response came mostly from S teachers. The idea that History is the central subject in much of the entire curriculum, the pivotal subject for much of the humanities and the social studies, was voiced by S, and to a lesser extent, M teachers. (Some of these respondents seemed to feel that history was the mother discipline for much of the humanities and the social studies, while others believed that history was simply the bridge between these two.) Interestingly, those teachers (about 3-4%, not tallied above) who specifically wrote that circumstances and time did not permit the integration of social studies and humanities via history or some other means, were largely S teachers also. It may be that those S teachers who consider themselves History teachers (see above) see the humanities and social studies as intrinsically joined in their own teaching, whereas those with different backgrounds may approve of this notion but find it not feasible to implement, given their own teaching approaches. Unfortunately, we cannot determine the extent to which our respondents truly considered or are sensitive to the total scope of the humanities, including literature and language, the arts, etc., in their schools and their teaching.

◆   A9   Additional remarks or topics you wish for the Commission to consider. Perhaps you would suggest the essential topics or courses for a good social studies curriculum.

Over 160 teachers (out of a possible 275) responded to this open-ended question. The proportion of E, M, and S teachers was approximately the same as in the Questionnaire A study population as a whole. A rough coding of their qualitative responses is as follows:

Social studies education is inseparable from the humanities. The understanding of man's past— social, economic, and political — depends upon an educated awareness of his expressions. (S - Louisiana)

History is very important to social studies and the others are minor players. (M - Kansas)

Type of response	% generating response
General characterization of good social studies	33.1
Sketch of ideal curriculum	19.0
Quality of teachers, teacher education, professional support	14.7
Emphasis on students' skill development	8.6
Textbooks	6.7
Interdisciplinary approach	3.7
Pedagogy, teachers' skills	1.2

Increase global education at all levels. It is too late to wait until grade six or seven to begin educating children about the larger world—foreign language instruction is also vital. (E - Nebraska)

Resist becoming a 'dumping ground' for every cause groups want to perpetuate—we cannot be competent to teach every social issue perceived as important by special-interest groups. (M - Colorado)

More public spending for projects encouraging teachers and students to bridge the space between the textbook and the real world. Use community resources to encourage real involvement by students. (M - Connecticut)

I believe that the social studies contribute to the total academic experience by encouraging students to acquire: the ability to grasp a question; the capacity to gather relevant data, to analyze it, to marshall pertinent arguments and to reach sound conclusions; the ability to communicate, both in oral and written expression; a quality of open-mindedness that is reflected in respect for another point of view, in tolerance for ambiguity, in passion for truth, and respect for facts; the ability to be sensitive to religious and ethical differences; the ability to make personal choices which are characterized by courage, dedication, and moral decisiveness. (S - Illinois)

Perhaps because so many of the preceding questions had focussed on specific curriculum aspects, the most typical response to this question—despite the wording of the second sentence—was a general description of the *tone* or *focus* or *character* of social studies in the schools. Leaving aside those responses that simply invoked goals like "good," "vital," etc. (these were relatively few), the most common emphasis—accounting for about half of the 33%—was on social studies' being up-to-date, relevant to contemporary concern, in touch with the multicultural nature of American society, and/or connected to the world as a whole. This kind of description came equally from the three teaching levels, E, M, and S.

Those who did comment largely on curriculum design were quite specific, recommending the number of courses, the level at which they should be taught, etc. These were overwhelmingly *secondary* teachers: a good 70% of those responding in this category were from the high school level. Their recommendations were fairly conventional or "academic," in that they focussed on more geography at the middle grades level, better coverage of world history, the importance of a social-science course like economics or social psychology (either as an elective or a requirement), the need for coverage of ancient history in the history sequence, etc.

Here again we seem to see a commitment to what might be called solid traditional social studies, expressed in terms of the enrichment or re-invigoration of the existing curriculum pattern, *together with* a strong "minority view," which, while not hostile to the traditional "academic" emphasis, wants more attention to global, multicultural, international, and contemporary material. When teachers are asked questions about "what is," their frame of reference is the former; when they comment on "what could be," many (by no means all) show the latter set of concerns.

Despite the importance assigned by teachers to students' acquiring the skills necessary for informed citizenship (cf. A6), only a few respondents to this question discussed this topic; almost all who did emphasized the general dimension of critical thinking. Despite a general endorsement of interdisciplinary relationships, especially with the humanities (cf. A4), very few emphasized this direction. Comments on textbooks, largely from S teachers, concerned the need for texts for specific courses and areas, and seldom concerned overall quality. Finally, although a number of M and S teachers focussed on intramural institutional or professional factors—school governance, departmental arrangements, teacher cooperation, etc.—very few respondents to this question concerned themselves with within-classroom teaching techniques, pedagogical improvement, and the like.

Questionnaire B: Approaches to Teaching

As stated above (p.37), the number of teachers responding to Questionnaire B was lower than that responding to the previous forms. For E teachers, the *n* for a particular question was 35 or less; except as noted below, they are often ignored in our discussion (although tallied in the tables).

◆   B1   What do you do best in teaching?

Type of response	% generating response
Pedagogical techniques	50.5
Stimulating, challenging students	13.0
Subject area proficiency	8.5
Academic skills proficiency	4.5
Social skills development	3.0

Among 200 respondents, about 100 cited the ability to manage class discussion, bring perspectives beyond that of the textbook to the material, or to teach flexibly depending on the topic. This type of response was somewhat more common among S teachers. The ability to motivate, stimulate, and challenge students was slightly more common among M than S teachers. Some teachers mentioned specific subject areas; others cited the ability to instill critical thinking or guide problem-solving; the latter responses came mostly from S teachers. Of the few who cited special ability in building self-worth, success with peers, etc., most were M teachers. In previous questions we have seen that S teachers have well-developed opinions and preferences about specific curriculum content, but this may partly reflect the fact that *courses* are better-defined in the high school. There is some evidence here (and elsewhere; see A6) that some S teachers also attend to "higher-order thinking" in their students, while M teachers are perhaps more likely to try to develop academic motivation, curiosity, and self-confidence.

◆   B2   What advantages/disadvantages do you see in grouping students according to ability. Does one outweigh the other?

Need teachers who can capture the imagination and teach concepts and skills—a fantastic curriculum on paper is not enough. (S - Vermont)

I am best at helping students reach higher levels of critical thinking through varied questioning strategies that emphasize a now and then approach. I challenge students to look at history as not merely a jumbled set of facts and concepts, but as a critical chain of events and causation that impacted history then, now, and in the future. (M - California)

Take advantage of teachable moments. Develop problem solving skills. Challenge fast learners. (E - Connecticut)

I relate well with kids and I'm flexible in my teaching so as to meet their needs and interests. I'm also open-minded to suggestions put to me by my kids. (M - Colorado)

Grouping by ability I have found to be a greater handicap than an advantage. The slow learner, by not being challenged and assisted by the other students, go only slower, sinking into the lowest common denominator. The more advanced students by middle school become egotistical, believing they know all there is to know. (M - California)

The advantages for the teacher are somewhat offset by the disadvantage to the student. (S - Michigan)

I believe that this is probably the foundation for the Social Studies. It sounds so simplistic, but it is extremely difficult to transfer this global objective into the classroom. (E - Illinois)

It's partly true; this is part of what we should be about. We should also be concerned with helping people more adequately make decisions by helping them learn how to make decisions and by providing a knowledge base for them to use in formulating decisions. Further helping students to understand themselves is part of what we should do. (M - Pennsylvania)

Type of response	% generating response
Disadvantageous to group	29.2
Grouping needed	26.2
Blend of both is best	7.9
No direct or clear answer	31.2

Although 202 teachers responded to this question, about one-third of them seemed to have no clear opinions: they *referred to* advantages or disadvantages, but did not make their own position or reasoning clear. Among these respondents, M and S teachers were about evenly split between Group, Don't Group, and No Clear Answer. E teachers were strongly (57%) for not grouping in social studies; even though the *n* was small, this result agrees with most other studies at the elementary level.

Among those clearly describing *why* grouping was advantageous, about 37 percent said that it was easier for teachers' planning and for the actual conduct of the class (for example, in classroom reading exercises). These reasons were relatively more common among E teachers. About 31 percent said that the students themselves were more *comfortable* when grouped by some form of ability or degree of readiness or preparation, and that thus "more success" was achieved by more students; about 20 percent said that such grouping was more *efficient* (more material could be covered in shorter time, relatively more attention could be given to every students).

Among those giving clear reasoning as to why grouping was disadvantageous, by far the dominant opinion (about 45%) was that with grouping less able (or less well prepared) students were prevented from in-class learning from the more able; about 23 percent cited ethical considerations; and about 12 percent commented that in ungrouped classrooms "able" and "less able" students learned from each other. In generating such responses, E, M, and S teachers were very much alike.

Thus, although opinion is roughly split among the A-R teachers about whether grouping is desirable, the *reasons for* grouping are more clearly conceptualized (not necessarily subscribed to) than the *reasons against.*

◆   B4   Please comment on or react to this statement. "Social studies in the schools should be the systematic study of people in societies in time and place."

This question was intended to see whether social studies teachers in our study population agreed, at least roughly, on a working definition of the field. (The suggested definition was drafted by a historian member of the Commission; the author's name was not given.)

Some responses were difficult to code: about 18 percent of the respondents either said they "disagreed," offered entirely different alternative definitions (which were diverse as a group), or were extremely equivocal. However, the proposed definition found a substantial degree of support.

Type of response	% generating response
Acceptable; agreed	44.9
Acceptable with specific additions	9.7
Too narrow	14.1
Too broad, vague	4.9
Trouble with term "systematic"	7.0

Unqualified agreement was obtained from the three teaching levels as follows: E, 26.9%; M, 30.4%; S, 58.4%. S teachers added specific elements—often mentioning the need for cross-subject integration or relating past to present—almost three times as often as M teachers. The bulk of the hesitations about the meaning of "systematic" came from E teachers, some of whom doubted that the exposition of material on their teaching level could do more than introduce or interest students in the subject matter. The response "Too narrow" came most heavily from M teachers (and to a lesser extent from S); the response "Too broad" (vague) was evenly distributed.

On further inspection, it appeared that most respondents who found the definition "too narrow" also proposed additional elements or considerations—as a group, essentially like those coded into the "Acceptable with additions" category. S teachers emphasized the need for interconnections with the humanities, and attention to the "experienced" life (rather than just the analysis or description) of human beings; they also stressed the interrelationship and interdependency of peoples and societies in the contemporary world, implying that the suggested definition was acceptable if it reflected such complexity. M teachers cited both these considerations, and were particularly interested in cross-subject and cross-department *integration*—i.e., in actual teaching, materials, and the like, including the natural world. They also emphasized building skills by means of which students could go beyond mere "content knowledge." (Cf. B1, where it was particularly S teachers who reported that they handled this aspect of teaching well.)

In sum, the definition appeared to be widely accepted as a minimal statement of the field, but to need some amplification, in practice at least. The prevalent concern with the interconnection of social studies, within themselves and to other parts of the curriculum, was illuminated further by answers to the next question.

This seems fair enough, provided that 'systematic' involves using the critical tools available to the historian, and that a variety of disciplines are involved. Economics, philosophy, psychology, history, political science, all must be involved in systematic. (M - New Jersey)

I would suggest that this statement does not go far enough —while the social studies is such, it must also include the interrelationships of societies and people. The interdependence of today's world must be stressed even when teaching about a given people and its society. (S - California)

By systematic, do you mean study of the institutions or systems? Or, do you mean a very structured study? I favor the first and oppose the second. (M - Colorado)

◆   B5   If you integrate or correlate various disciplines with your social studies course or topics, please describe and give examples.

Nature of the integration/correlation	% generating the description
The various social sciences	27.2
Literature	16.8
Writing, language arts	15.2
The arts, religion, philosophy	13.6

Under the "social sciences," the most common references were to aspects of economics, geography, political science, sociology. (There were also comments by perhaps 10 percent of the respondents involving human relations and behavior, both anthropological and psychological.) In apparent contrast to some comments in replies to B4, there were very few citations of interrelationship with the natural sciences (other than in geography).

Reports of integration or cross-relation *within* the social sciences, or of the correlation of "other" social science concepts and approaches with a largely historical exposition, came two and three times as often from S teachers as from M and E, respectively. (This is not due to the disproportion of S teachers in the Questionnaire B respondent group.) It is an interesting result, given the fact that discipline-based courses are most prevalent in secondary schools, whereas curriculum guides and policies for E and M often describe "integrated" or "fused" content approaches.

In consonance with B4, the citation of writing, English grammar, or other aspects of language use was conceived of as a *skill*, to be closely connected to and practiced in social studies content work. By contrast, literature, the arts, religion, and philosophy involved texts, artifacts, and concepts as abstract *entities* which social studies should capture or recognize. Both kinds of mentions came about equally from E, M, and S teachers, although writing *per se* was specially prominent among M teachers.

In a related question (not tallied here), teachers who tried to integrate and correlate across subjects were asked their over-all strategy or means for doing so. Responses from S teachers did not form a coherent pattern. Among M teachers, the typical means was for one subject—generally, history or geography—to be the core material, with other concepts and approaches correlated to it. Again, it appears from this study group that social studies "fusion" in the middle grades is less the rule than curriculum theory suggests.

◆   B6   What are the major dilemmas you face in organizing a world history program or course?

World Studies incorporates history, sociology, economics, geography, as does U. S. History. (S - Illinois)

I'm always relating reading, literature and music to social studies. Reading The courage of Anne Noble *and discussing early settlement of Connecticut and Indians in Ct in the early 1700's. (E - Connecticut)*

American history and American literature are taught at the same grade level. Through slides, videos, projects, we see the arts, architecture, dance, music, etc. (S - Louisiana)

Type of response	% generating response
Too much to cover	29.9
What to select, how make relevant	18.4
Time constraints	11.6
Materials	6.8

Of the 58 M and 78 S teachers responding to this question, almost 69 percent said, in one way or another, that the subject was so vast that it could only be dipped into rather than organized. About 30 percent emphasized the arbitrariness of choosing some periods and areas within world history, while another 18 percent focussed more on how to connect the material selected to the present time and place. The latter response was more typical of S teachers. Very few teachers mentioned any lack of preparation to teach the subject—which is interesting, since other research shows that few teachers have taken much world or regional history. But some teachers, particularly M teachers, reported that the available books and materials did not work for students with varying levels of ability and varying interests.

In a related open-ended question (not tallied here), 8 percent of those teachers who reported experience in teaching world history said that a thematic approach, rather than a chronological and/or areal approach, could be effective; 6 percent favored the latter approach. Nearly 20 percent found that team teaching, class or group projects, or student research methods—something beyond straight lecturing and text study—was needed.

◆ B7 What are the major dilemmas you face in organizing an American history program or course?

Type of response	% generating response
Time constraints, too much to cover	37.6
Focus and sequencing	16.3

Among the 59 M and 74 S teachers responding, the dilemmas cited were somewhat different from those reported in world history. Teachers were not puzzled by *what* to cover—in the sense of the appropriate time period or venue—so much as frustrated in what to select *within* the over-all subject. There was also concern with how to focus a particular level of American history teaching, given the presence of similar courses at other grade levels, and how to build continuity across exposures. There were no differences between M and S teachers in these regards.

Proportionately more S teachers reported a "dilemma" vis-à-vis the chronological vs the thematic approach, but the *n*s were too small to put much weight on this aspect of these data.

Insisting on at least a 2-year course of study is essential. Anything else is a mockery. (S - Kentucky)

We often say 'World History' and it ends up being a study of politics and governments of Western Civilizations. Little is studied about the everyday life of 90% of the population. (E - Illinois)

The major dilemma I have with American history is, Do we follow the major text and study politics and wars, or do we study periods of time which will include every aspect of people's lives? If we do this we'll never cover Discovery to the Present. (E - Illinois)

Perhaps my major dilemma is how to strike a proper balance between scholarly precision, thoroughness and attention to details, and emphasizing the larger overarching themes and questions from America's heritage. Sometimes I become too detail-oriented and lose sight of the larger picture. (M - New Jersey)

When asked to report in an open-ended fashion their own experiences in teaching American history, the most common report among the M teachers who complied was that the topical/thematic approach was more effective than the chronological; among S teachers, this was reversed. (There was a strong minority opinion at each of the two levels on this matter.) Both M and S teachers agreed that keeping student interest, making the material "come alive," was a problem.

◆   B8   What are the major dilemmas you face in organizing a geography program or course?

Interpretable responses here came from 15 E, 57 M, and 56 S teachers.

Type of response	% generating response
Finding the right materials	13.1
Time constraints; too much to cover	12.3
Lack of student skills, knowledge	11.5
Other substantive comments	36.2

Lack of hands-on materials for students. (E - Virginia)

I teach on a small island where most of my students have always lived. They have great difficulty perceiving location, directions, or of a world outside their own. (E - South Carolina)

Time and topic selection is critical. It is virtually impossible to teach a comprehensive world geography course in one semester. (S - Mississippi)

A problem with materials was most common among E teachers, and had to do with the developmental level, texts versus supplementary materials, and the need for diverse "hands-on" materials in the classroom. The problem of too much to cover in too little time was also most prominent among E teachers; there may be an interaction here, in that adequate "coverage" at this level may depend on the use of effective materials. The level of skills and preparation among students was a problem about equally for M and S teachers. (The fact that 11.5 percent of the respondents cited this dilemma is noteworthy when we consider that only 1.4 percent cited lack of skills and knowledge in connection with American history.)

This question had an unusually large proportion of responses that were meaningful and appropriate to the question, but very hard to categorize. Looking further into this diversity of responses, we found that M teachers (in this Other Substantive category) most often talked about the *integration* of geography into other courses or with other content. Some teachers found such integration a problem: "Geography out of context, without history or current events, doesn't seem to stick." Others, however, found that geography was *so well integrated* that the dilemma, if any, was in giving it a separate identity: "Geography is integrated into my history/social studies courses, so this question doesn't really apply"; "How to integrate geography into course content without organizing a separate unit *to teach basic geographic literacy*" (emphasis added).

Some of the same questions were raised by S teachers—e.g., "Integrating geography into the other courses and still have it *taught*" (emphasis in the original). Some S teachers also referred to the problem of Someone should do it, but who? "We don't have a required geography course and experience difficulty making certain that geographic concepts and skills are incorporated into other courses." These comments, together with similar ones from M teachers, generally revolve around the question of separate exposition of geography versus its "infusion" elsewhere.

In addition, however, S teachers grappled with the definition of what *kind* of geography should be taught. "What is considered Geography and what is Earth Science?" "The text is very place-oriented, short chapters dealing with location, climate, resources, and industry. My dilemma is lack of cultural geography." It is interesting to note that the same indecision about the appropriate *nature* of the subject matter is not reported, for example, in connection with world history (though it may be true in the university). That is, our A-R teachers reported many dilemmas with selection and focus in world history, but not dilemmas of what form world history should take (i.e., political vs cultural or demographic, relationship between human and physical aspects, etc.)

◆   B9   Is there planned repetition (i.e., American history in grades 5, 8, 11) in the curriculum you follow?
          Does it work well, adequately, or poorly? (Answer in relation to content and/or skill.)

About 160 teachers responded to these paired questions. Some 70 percent reported the *presence* of planned repetition (about 7 percent reported that there was none; about 23 percent were unclear or equivocal). In judging whether such repetition *worked well*, nearly 38 percent gave no (or no interpretable) answer. Presumably this included teachers in those systems where repetition was absent. More important, by far the highest number of nonresponders were E teachers, many of whom may not be in a position to know, at least in detail, *how well* repetition of history works at higher grade levels. If E teachers are removed from the calculations, the proportion of nonresponders drops to 10 percent.

Among those with clear opinions, 29.3 percent said *Poorly*, 11.5 percent said *Well*, and 10.8 percent said *Adequately*. Apparently, planned repetition is by far the prevalent pattern; and apparently it is not regarded as a great success.

In addition to failing frequently to give a judgment at all, E teachers who did so were by a considerable margin the most satisfied, at least superficially. Even here, however, many were of two minds or tentative—for example, approving of the intent of planned repetition and "spiralling," but unsure of how well it worked in practice. "There is [a plan] and I approve of it. At least in theory, students should deepen their understanding of the material in studying it again when they are older."

Middle and secondary school responses fell more heavily into the "poor" category—about four "poorly" to one "well." Middle school teachers tended to mention that there were too many gaps in the curriculum (that is too many important topics left out entirely, such as "the repeated study of American history at the expense of other disciplines such as world history"). A chief concern at both levels was that "planned" repetition was in fact verbatim repetition; the same general material is taught over and over, or at least students perceive it that way.

There is, and I approve of it. At least in theory, students should deepen their understanding of the materials by studying it again when they are older. (E - New York)

As well as can be expected. While math and English use daily repetition through many years, we introduce material for the first time, repeat it once four years later and wonder that everybody does not remember everything. (M - Michigan)

In-service education (paid), 2) time available for sharing, 3) adequate texts and supplies, 4) teaching space adequate for class size, 5) administrative support the value of the subject. (E - Missouri)

Mentioned by both groups, but more common at the secondary level, was belief that there is little retention of what had been learned before. Of particular concern was that American history is traditionally taught three times at widely separated intervals. Although some teachers believe a partial way to solve the problem would be for the focus of content to be markedly different at each level, others (who may work in schools that do divide the content up so that students will not have a survey course three times in their school career), see the problem differently. Their concern was two-fold: not only did they agree that the interval—5th to 8th grade and 8th to 11 grade—was too long for general retention, but they were most concerned that splitting the course material, even with "review" materials built in, means that students do not have the opportunity to spend sufficient time on key periods of history when they are at a more sophisticated level of understanding.

For secondary teachers, another situation caused problems. There may be, on paper, a designed program for sequential planned repetition, but many high schools have a number of feeder schools and cannot count on students having the same preparation. "Everyone arrives here with variations on a similar background."

◆   B10   List the working conditions you need to become a better professional. Try to prioritize the list.

About 190 (out of a possible 247) teachers responded to the question, as follows.

Type of response	% generating response
Inservice education, professional growth programs	19.5
Administrative support and commitment, congenial atmosphere, professional autonomy	19.5
Adequate materials (including supplementary)	9.5
Smaller class size, better classroom conditions	8.4
Sharing, team teaching	6.3
Ability grouping	.5
Other	21.1

There's repetition, but it is poorly planned and doesn't occur uniformly across the district. Many people feel that the repetition is causing students to become disinterested in American History in upper grades. Secondly, many question the repeated study of American History at the expense of other disciplines, e.g., World History. (M - Colorado)

Although the two top response categories were equal, those who cited inservice education, etc., were heavily E teachers; those citing administrative support and professional conditions tended also to be E teachers, but less disproportionately so. *It should not be concluded that E teachers in general are the most dissatisfied*: only 13 E teachers in the A-R group replied, and it is possible to assume that those who did were ones who were unhappy. Among M and S teachers, and in other areas of concern, there were no marked differences across teaching levels.

Answers to this question provided useful cross-checks on some other results in this study. For example, as against the results obtained in B2, where teachers provided coherent opinions about grouping, the fact is that on this question very few teachers saw this as a major factor in their immediate professional lives. Similarly, very few teachers had cited inadequate education or preparation for teaching history and geography (see B6, B7, B8), and the A-R teachers have not previously expressed problems with pedagogy (see CP10 and B1); yet a substantial proportion responding to this question cited the need for continuing inservice education and training. It is not clear from the written responses, but it is possible that what the A-R teachers want out of inservice training is neither subject-specific methodology nor general pedagogical principles, but professional enrichment, dignity, attention, and a sense of growth. In that case, the two top response categories for this question are facets of the same dimension.

On the other hand, qualitative judgments of the "Other" responses show two frequent themes, running through all teaching levels: first, the desire for *respect for the field of social studies*, and, second, a great concern for lack of time.

A curriculum that makes sense! One in which students learn skills, reinforce them, and learn content in a logical, sequential way; 2) materials written for the middle school—I'm so weary of rewriting everything;...3) greater opportunity for exemplary units to be shared with other teachers across the country;...4) alternative forms of evaluation/appraisal other then traditional pencil/paper tests. (M - Colorado)

———

Desirable working conditions would include: 1) more opportunities to share ideas/knowledge/ resources/activities with colleagues, both at our own teaching level and at other levels; 2) more opportunities to attend lectures on specific social studies topics (including specific history topics); 3) more night classes available in specific content areas, not just in the field of education. (S - West Virginia)

———

5. Images of the Present and the Future in Social Studies

As indicated on p. 7 and p. 18, we have reserved presentation and discussion of two portions of the data for this concluding section. In the Community Profile, teachers were asked to describe what they saw as the strengths and weaknesses of the social studies programs they were most familiar with. In the Teacher Profile, some months later, they were asked to write in an open-ended fashion about what they would want social studies to be in the future. The similarities that are evident across these two questions provide a picture, taken from those now in the system, of how to get there from here—of the implicit or intended dynamics of the present evolution of field. The qualifications— "implicit," "intended"—simply mean that such an evolution is not determined. Outside events or influences—new educational thinking, a change in the political climate or the civic culture, the impact of reform movements—would alter the process. Even if such external factors were absent, so that what appears to be a natural trend as of today continued, conditions within and outside the system—the level of educational financing, the training and morale of teachers, the governance of schools, and even such matters as the nature of texts and tests—might well slow or terminate such movement.

Here, then, are two snapshots, of today and tomorrow, taken from the same vantage point.

◆   CP 10   Please describe what you feel to be the strength and the weakness of your current social studies program.

Responses to this question were provided by 173 persons:

Elementary - 22; Middle - 30; Secondary - 87; Supervisors/administrators - 34[19]

Answers to this open-ended question were wide-ranging, thoughtful, and often lengthy or complex. Most respondents discussed at least three or four "strengths" and three or four "weaknesses." To facilitate analysis, the total number of responses from the entire group responding were separated into three general headings: Curriculum, Curriculum Related, and Teachers/Teaching.

Mentions of Specific Concerns (N=720)

Curriculum		**Curriculum Related**	
General Quality	98	Instruc. Materials	62
History Program	35	Coordination	79
Requirements	28	Methodologies	35
Electives	26	Skills	17
		Testing	13
Geography	20	Need for Depth	10
U.S. History	11	Innovation	5
Social Sciences	11		
Humanities	11		221
World History	9		
Global Studies	13		
Contemporary Issues	8		
	270		

Teachers/Teaching	
Quality of Teachers	85
Professional Growth	47
Academic Freedom	30
Funding	46
Community Support	21
	229

Curriculum

Quality and Organization

Middle and secondary teachers were about evenly divided on the general quality of their schools' programs. Half felt their program was working toward sound goals and objectives and was properly sequenced and articulated. The other half, who criticized the quality of the curriculum, tended to emphasize lack of continuity or logical focus. A typical statement points up the problem: "On paper, program district wide is fairly solid; no standardization or uniformity in practice. Breaks down into a hodge-podge of offerings...."

Elementary teachers were the least satisfied. More than three-fourths believed their program lacked focus and had suffered as the result of recent emphasis on basic skills of reading, writing, and computation. Several described the need for social studies curriculum guidelines and many complained of the lack of time devoted to the subject.

Requirements and Electives

Across all levels, respondents believed—nearly two to one—that present requirements were inadequate. Along with insufficient time allotted at the early elementary grade level, some noted that students took no social studies in particular grades, 5 or 6 or 8, or that only three years were required in high

In surveys, 60% of the students indicate this area to be a 'least favorite' subject. They find it questionable as to how much relevance it will have in their lives. (M - Maine)

Heavy emphasis on the importance and significance of social studies in all grades K-12; a generally favorable attitude on the part of students toward social studies— over 80% of the seniors electing social studies beyond the requirements of the state or the district; much teacher input into the on-going development for the program. (M - Missouri)

At the elementary level the social studies do not receive a high priority. For example, children with low reading levels are often removed from social studies to attend reading classes. (E - Oklahoma)

Little change in curriculum since 1918; no world history, non-western history, psychology, sociology, geography. (S - Minnesota)

school. On the other hand, a number of teachers commented on the strong elective program in their school, and a few mentioned that more electives ought to be offered.

The Subject Matters

We have a chrono-topical approach to teaching U.S. history which gives us time to incorporate other fields of social studies, to teach process as well as content, to assist students with thinking development, as well as know U.S. history. (S - Illinois)

Respondents were far more positive about the quality of the history program than of programs for any other social studies disciplines. Those who mentioned problems concentrated on the lack of depth in studies of recent history and difficulties in finding time to increase offerings in non-Western history without diluting strong programs in traditional Western history. The most common complaint was that there was too much content and too little time.

There is a heavy emphasis on the traditional Western-oriented curriculum. We are trying to increase non-Western offerings without diluting the impact of what we already do well. (S - Massachusetts)

More than 80% of the respondents who discussed the subject of geography stressed the need for more and better geography content. Only 11 respondents mentioned the other social sciences; of those, five believed more economics should be included in the curriculum, one would have both economics and government taught at the end of the student's school career, and the others described strong programs in the behavioral sciences.

Simplistic geography strand. Too much teaching about maps and not enough use of geographic information to find out about people and places. (E - Oregon)

Slightly over half of the teachers touching on global studies or contemporary issues felt their schools were doing a good job in those areas, but all 11 respondents describing humanities/interdisciplinary courses were enthusiastic about the quality of the offerings and suggested the need for more such courses throughout the K-12 grades. Several did mention the demands on teachers' time that such courses represent.

Curriculum Related

Instructional Materials (cf TP 17)

In a small school, the scheduling problems and conflicts find English, Math, and Science given first consideration and you get what is left over for social studies courses. (S - Nebraska)

The quality of instructional materials and equipment received a good deal of praise by respondents. Many commented that school and school district media centers were well stocked and well used. Several mentioned a regular, efficient adoption cycle for textbooks and only two complained about a poor process for purchase of materials. Comments on the quality of textbooks were also positive except for those used for grades 1-3. There were some rather chilling statements, however. Some respondents were pleased that they now had a textbook for every student. Others were concerned that maps remained out-of-date, and several spoke of the lack of computers for students' use.

Coordination of Instruction

We do have a strong secondary supervisor who is trying to bring...out of the Dark Ages. Many, many challenges in this state. (M-...)

Several secondary teachers addressed the functioning of the social studies department. Most were complimentary about the management abilities of their department chair and praised the chair's efforts to keep them informed about activities within the district as well as "happenings throughout the country."

School administrators, particularly principals, fared less well. Nearly half of the respondents writing on this topic praised their principal's efforts in managing the school building and their supportive and cooperative attitudes, but slightly more than half were sharply critical of their principal. The critics cited lack of interest in the academic program, no effort to build schedules that would allow team teachers common planning time, not being in charge, and making no effort to provide needed inservice programs.

Although there were some comments that curriculum specialists were not as well qualified to hold their jobs as they might be, the greatest number of remarks concerning the school district's social studies coordinator were positive. Several respondents noted that the coordinator was overworked or was responsible for too many duties. Others, mostly from small school systems, noted that there was no coordinator, although one was badly needed.

One person to work with social studies, grades K-12, in 119 schools. (K-12 - Tennessee)

Methodologies

Thirty-five respondents described methodologies that they felt supported content learning. Among the most frequently mentioned methods or activities were cooperative learning, independent study opportunities, attention to learning styles, participatory programs such as History Day and Model U.N.'s, and use of local resources. Useful structures for presenting the curriculum also received a number of comments—particularly the use of flexible-modular scheduling which allows for efficient use of instructional time, and schemes for grouping students that helps all of them achieve the same learning objectives. Two-thirds of the mentions on these topics were positive. The negative comments were usually phrased to indicate the need for these methodologies to be actually (or more fully) implemented.

Strong, on-going programs that provide participatory opportunities for students (Projects Fair, Model Metro Government Day, Voter Registration Program, Academic Olympics). (K-12 - Tennessee)

Skills and Testing (cf TP 15)

Teachers were about evenly divided in describing the schools' skills development programs and testing programs as a strength or a weakness. Those who cited strong skills programs specifically mentioned the teaching of writing skills, critical thinking, group process, decision making, conflict resolution, and computer skills. Those who described testing as a strength stated that analyzing down test items helped to identify problems in knowledge areas as well as the capability to identify problems encountered by individual students.

A strength of our program is the use of computer software to develop and reinforce social studies understanding. We have one computer per 17 students. (S - Wyoming)

Those who felt skills development to be a weakness referred to lack of sequencing in teaching skills and indicated that the teaching of higher order skills took time away from teaching content—and it was content that the "too many" tests were based upon. Reasons given for citing testing as a weakness were that too often the tests did not bear close, or any, relationship to the curriculum. Mentioned most frequently as poorly designed were criterion referenced tests, essential elements tests, and performance objective tests— the very tests that are supposed to be most closely tied to mandated curriculum. Respondents were also critical of the quality of tests purporting to measure *pre* and *post* gains in cognitive understanding, values development, and skills development. Although relatively few respondents wrote on these two topics, both skills and testing appear to be areas of contention.

Thinking skills are espoused, but because of the criterion-referenced test, teachers forego teaching higher level thinking to teach facts that the test measures. (E - Massachusetts)

Need for Depth; Need for Innovation

So few teachers wrote on these two topics that they might simply have been combined in an "Other" category. However, the responses highlight concerns that were expressed more fully in other questions. The general consensus is that there is too much content to cover and too little time allotted for students to do in-depth analysis of what they do study. At the same time, respondents indicated that they could not choose what ought to be left out of a K-12

Our district is open to innovation. We have heard several national authorities and have been sent out to see what others are doing. (M - Colorado) curriculum. Those who wrote of innovative programs mentioned the need to experiment with combining subject matters and to discontinue repetitive course work. "Utilize national trends," suggested one respondent.

Teachers and Teaching

Quality of Teachers (cf TP 4)

The largest number of respondents writing on any single topic, in this area, discussed the quality of teachers as either a strength or a weakness. Of the 85 responses, there were 52 unequivocally positive statements. Terms such as well-trained, enthusiastic, and committed appeared over and over. Of the 33 responses that considered the teaching staff as a weakness, the majority described their colleagues as unable to accept new ideas, "hide-bound," or waiting to retire. A small group of respondents (13) felt the large number of coaches in their department to be a weakness, citing both unwarranted preference given in hiring and that the time spent in coaching interfered with effective classroom teaching. It should be noted that the latter problem was cited by both coaches and non-coaches.

Professional Growth (cf CP 6d, CP 9, B 10)

Perhaps the most critical comments on this question relate to either poor or non-existent district-provided opportunities for professional growth. In the ratio of five to one, respondents mentioned "lack of staff development" or "no methods for identifying weak instruction and improving these teachers." Of those who did comment that the school system had an extensive professional growth and staff development program, many were dissatisfied with the particular individual who handles the program and others expressed disgust toward their fellow teachers who did not take advantage of opportunities provided. Several commented that inservice programs would be better received if they related more directly to content areas rather than to "generic" topics such as classroom management skills or techniques for classroom questioning.

Academic Freedom (cf TP 10-11)

Teachers in this sample feel strongly that, on the whole, they have a great deal of academic freedom. They mentioned their flexibility to follow curriculum goals using their own pattern, their ability to select teaching materials appropriate to their classes, and the fact that no one was looking over their shoulder. On the other hand, several mentioned frustration at not being in a decision making position about what is taught and when it is taught, the scope and sequence of the curriculum.

Funding and Teaching Conditions (cf B 10)

Teaching conditions are inextricably tied up with questions of funding. Insufficient funding was listed as the cause of too large classes, lack of good teaching materials, few or inadequate inservices for teachers, insufficient teaching space, poorly equipped classrooms, insufficient heat or air conditioning, and low teacher salaries.

In our school, we have excellent teachers teaching social studies. Our department is the best in our school. (S - Florida)

The greatest strength of the district is the quality and dedication of the teachers it is able to attract. (S - Arizona)

Declining student enrollments have resulted in fewer and fewer young teachers joining our system. As a result, the challenge that comes with new members to the teaching community has been lost. We are sometimes too comfortable with one another and need the infusion of creative approaches to shake up our day to day department activities. (S - Nebraska)

Community Support

On the whole, respondents wrote of good community support for the schools. Several reported climates supportive of innovation, the teaching of controversial issues. A number of respondents also indicated that community businesses supported the schools. A few respondents noted little public support or unwarranted interference by community members, suggesting that special interest groups had forced their own causes onto the schools and "cluttered up the curriculum."

◆ TP 18. What is your vision of effective, useful social studies instruction for students who will spend most of their lives in the 21st century?

Elementary - 130; Middle - 166; Secondary - 295   T=591

As might be expected, such a broad question brought lengthy answers that addressed multiple concerns. In terms of focus of concerns, the patterns of responses to TP18 was quite consonant with those of responses to CP10, although the questionnaires were completed some months apart in time. The areas that evoked the fullest comments were (a) curriculum content, (b) curriculum-related matters such as building subject-related skills, and (c) teaching conditions, broadly considered. (Many more teachers, however, took the time to respond to a question about the future than to characterize the present reality.)

Content Regarded as Important

Number of mentions: 990

	Elementary	Middle	Secondary	Totals
U. S. History	13	31	66	110
History (not specified)	9	25	73	107
World History	3	33	37	73
Government/Civics/Law	37	74	111	222
Global/Other Cultures	50	55	63	168
Geography	33	34	57	124
Contemporary Issues	19	26	54	99
Economics	4	4	25	33
Other (Intergroup Relations, Expanding Horizons, Being Human)	10	2	13	25
Behavioral Sciences	0	0	22	22
Social Sciences (not specified)	0	5	9	14
	178	289	530	990

The teachers discussing content clearly expressed a commitment to the traditional subjects of history and government, but the ranking of global and crosscultural studies is suggestive. Mentions of history taken together total 290,

Bigness is a major enemy of education because it forces conformity and routine in order to maintain order and the status quo. Schools (at least ours) seem more concerned about getting students into good colleges and universities than education. Students learn to value grades and class rank, and meaningful decision-making seems limited to choice of electives. (S - Illinois)

While 'critical thinking skills' are in disrepute at the moment, because of popular impression and the worst practices which separate skills and content, much value and good sense lie at the base of the goal of teaching students to think. (S - Illinois)

Children prepared to live in the 21st century need the same kinds of social studies instruction as my generation and my ancestors' generations needed. Technologies and environments change, but human nature changes very little, if at all. Social studies instruction for the future, any future, needs to emphasize those skills, knowledge, and values that will confer the ability to cope with one's world. (E - Indiana)

Students must learn to be active participants in the learning process. They need to learn to "make connections"—to use critical thinking skills to become wise decision makers; to value the democratic process—know it and support it "with clear eyes"; to be able to see both sides of an argument, but be able to take a stand and support that stand with evidence, not emotions. They should care about and be willing to support their democracy. (M - Missouri)

For the 21st century, citizens will need a grasp of where to find and how to interpret a wide variety of data. They need to know how to influence their world and have enough hope to try to do so. (S - California)

Teachers can teach history, geography, political science right out of the many texts they now use if they only realize that all aspects of life are related to the social sciences. Working together to build a cumulative effect, rather than a repetitive effect, we can give students an education that does prepare them for the challenges they'll face in becoming productive adults. (M - New Jersey)

the highest number for any of the disciplines. However, unlike the results of question A7 asking what content is essential to achieving the purpose of social studies education (see p. 43), the rank order thereafter changes. Government/civics/law and global/crosscultural studies precede geography in ranking.

Some of this difference may be traced to statistical factors. In A7, 251 teachers generated some 1545 content mentions, but for each of the three teaching levels. Here, in TP18, more teachers have generated fewer content mentions, and with no particular reference to the question of what content should be taught where. Given these facts, and the wording of the question itself, it is reasonable to suggest that teachers responding to TP18 gave more personally salient recommendations than those responding to A7. These are teachers describing, not What is, but What should be.

There is a further difference in the wording of and context for the two questions. In A7, teachers were asked what is the essential content to achieve the main purpose of social studies education. This question, TP18, asked about an effective, useful social studies program for students who will live in the 21st century. It is reasonable, again, to suppose that some teachers, in the former case, were describing what fits today, given a well-understood essential purpose, but in the latter case were assuming a modified or broadened central purpose—for example, a version of citizenship extended into a world of more highly integrated and interdependent societies.

Our interpretation of the comments made by many or most of the teachers who wrote most fully about the need for greater understanding of all the world's people, their ways of life and cultural beliefs, is that they had in mind particularly that content typically contained in cultural geography coursework. In A7, it appeared that Geography should be distinguished from Global/Cross-Cultural; i.e., that the former indicated primarily geography as spatial distribution and location, rather than as a facet of the study of human life *in situ* and in culture. (The two are, of course, not in conflict, but in school courses there are marked differences in emphasis.)

If the categories of global/other cultures and geography are combined, the total is 292, about the same number of mentions as for history. However, many of the comments focussing on other cultures, systems, and traditions emphasized strongly *the historical dimension*. In fact, we observe that in these data some of the citations of Geography, Global/Cross-Cultural, and World History all converge on the same desire: greater knowledge about the world outside the United States, in its contemporary and historical complexity.

Readers comparing TP18 with A7 will note that, in the former, the teachers have emphasized relatively more the study of government, civics, and law—all of these with a basically domestic focus. This would perhaps argue against our interpretation directly above. However, the relatively low rank assigned these content fields in A7 was associated (in qualitative analysis of the responses) with some tendency to hold that the essentials of enlightened American citizenship, through education, could be conveyed through the study of American History. It is not illogical to suppose that the teachers who look, for the future, to a more global approach to the curriculum in general may believe that "citizenship" in the future will not be completely explicated through American History, and that the direct study of government(s), law, and a less parochial form of civics will be needed. We cannot speculate further about this rather confusing aspect of these data, and can only urge that other studies look more deeply into them.

Curriculum-Related Concerns

Number of mentions: 601

	Elementary	Middle	Secondary	Total
Skills Development	75	121	187	383
Need for Integrated Curric.	16	17	61	94
Need to Teach Values/Ethics	7	22	55	84
Need for Depth over Coverage	7	10	23	40
	105	170	326	601

The most frequently mentioned item in this category was skills development. Although a few teachers mentioned basic skills such as reading with competence or using an atlas efficiently, the great majority described abilities requiring analysis and synthesis—problem solving, decision making, generating and testing hypotheses—and life management skills—conflict resolution, negotiation, participation in local, national, and international affairs. Learning activities that teachers mentioned in relation to skills development included field trips, computer simulations and graphing, a wide variety of writing assignments, debates, mock trials, and group projects. Said one teacher, "We need ways of structuring the learning programs that provide direct opportunities on a regular basis for active participation on a variety of levels for students. Passive students are unlikely to become active adults."

Some 94 teachers spoke to their concerns over what they see as a "fractured" curriculum. Both the humanities—art, philosophy, literature, music, religion—and the fields of science and technology were mentioned as important components of a good social studies program, and some teachers went beyond the typical infusion model, that is, including those items in a history course, to suggest that all typically prescribed school subjects be combined into grand multidisciplinary courses. Many of the teachers emphasizing the need for an integrated curriculum also stressed the need for greater, more overt, teaching of values and ethics. These may not be simply the traditional values of American education, however. Many of those writing about the need for more understanding of the entire world, i.e., global studies, also described the need for more attention to be paid to values and ethics. Some dozen or so underscored the responsibility of all humans to act as stewards for all the world's peoples and their lands.

Although only 40 teachers directly used the term "depth vs. coverage" others support the concept: e.g., many would abolish the usual three survey courses of U.S. history at grades 5, 8, and 11 and would replace it with a one-time two year

Perhaps most important to me is to open students' minds to the diversity of cultures and civilizations in the world. Useful social studies instruction teaches that not everywhere on earth is America. We must lead our students to the liberal values of tolerance and appreciation for diversity and beauty in the world, and to a rejection of ethnocentrism. We must teach more about the way other people live, because the more you know about other peoples' way of life, the more you know about yourself. (E - New York)

Social studies must involve values articulation. It's discouraging to see young people in corporate America consider only profits and assets. We must go back, or perhaps forward, to the values of loyalty to one's fellow men, decency, honesty and integrity toward others...I would urge a focus on things, people and events relating to the persisting ethical questions of mankind. Learners should be probing for themselves what it is to be a man or a woman. (S - Oregon) sequence that moved more slowly through the national chronology. Others wrote of the need to take more class time for students "to worry around a topic rather then whiz through."

Teaching Conditions

Finally, a large number of teachers' "visions" focussed on teaching (and learning) conditions, teacher empowerment, and professional autonomy.

Number of mentions: 192

Elementary	Middle	Secondary	Total
44	57	91	192

To accomplish my vision, the first thing that would have to happen is for teachers to have adequate planning time, especially time with other teachers, both within the field and in other fields. (S - Colorado)

Are we teachers or social workers? If we are to be social workers, counselors, etc., help those who don't want to do this find other jobs. For those teachers who want to go in this new direction, help them learn how. (M - New Jersey)

Clearly, teaching conditions that trouble teachers the most are lack of time, lack of teaching materials, and lack of money for teaching activities such as field trips. The majority of those complaining of lack of time indicated that they were expected to teach too many different subjects (elementary and secondary), were expected to handle too many non-teaching activities (middle school), or were too heavily burdened with papers and tests to be graded (secondary). The most frequently mentioned set of materials in short supply were computers and computer software. Several teachers felt that the society of the future would rely far more on the new technologies, but that the schools were lagging far behind industry and business, and were, in effect, training students to live in the past—not even the present. One teacher even wrote that she hoped schools of the future would provide a *typewriter* for every department office.

Many visions expressed the need for school design and scheduling that would allow students to become more responsible for their own learning. They emphasized the need for cooperative learning as well as greater use of computers, but they also indicated that much learning could best be achieved outside the school building. Although many simply stated the need for more field trips, others wrote lengthy commentaries on the need for first-hand student research that could be supplemented back in the classroom.

The need for greater teacher empowerment—in this case, their ability to make curricular decisions that affect their own students—was forthrightly stated by a few teachers, but alluded to by many others. What the teachers perceived as problem areas were state mandates for competency testing which forced coverage rather than understanding, insensitivity to the need for teachers' schedules to facilitate team and departmental planning, all-school schedules that prohibited field trips or even the viewing of a full one-hour film or a full classroom debate; in other words, the typical five or six period classes, five days a week, prevented the use of good teaching techniques. A continuation of these patterns (in some respects accelerating trends, as in competency testing) was seen by many teachers as prefiguring a rather dismal future for public education. On the other hand, there were several mentions of the importance of teachers taking part in scheduling, with several citations of good plans such as flexible-modular scheduling and the Sizer plan for essential learning.

It is unlikely that the most alienated of the A-R teachers took the trouble to respond to TP18. It is therefore reassuring that the number of responses was as high as it was. Although many anxieties were expressed in the visions, the majority of the responses were forward-looking. They stressed the need for schools to take in to account the changing society—the nature of the experiences students bring to the classroom with them, the validity of the traditional subjects, but also the need for greater understanding of the influences of the newer forms of communication and information exchange, and the greater sense of being part of a rapidly shrinking world.

For the sake of our nation, it is to be hoped that these teachers and others like them will receive the support they so richly deserve. Ernest Boyer's call for teacher empowerment must be taken to heart by all who care about our schools:

> Teaching is a gruelling, thankless job. Most people who criticize teachers could not long survive in many of the nation's schools...If we want better schools, this nation must find ways to identify great teachers and give them the recognition and the opportunities for renewal they deserve.[20]

Demand that schools hire the best teachers. demand that teachers be treated with respect. Reject mediocrity...help make the teaching of history a respected art rather than a necessary evil. (M - Vermont)

Endnotes

[1]   Available from the sponsoring organizations

[2]   Macmillan Publishing Co., 866 Third Avenue, New York 10022

[3]   Throughout this report we use means as a suitable average measure. Since we assume that our A-R respondents are *not* necessarily representative of a national population of teachers—either with respect to their relationship to social studies or other aspects—there is no reason to use median or modal value. The first would probably tend to bring our results closer to a representative national group of teachers; the second might accentuate the fact that our teachers are self-selected and in some respects unusual. In some questions, where our A-R teachers do look like a known national norm, we point that out.

[4]   New York: Charles Scribner's Sons, 1932.

[5]   We use the term "system" to refer to the particular legal-institutional educational entities: in some locales, for example, there will be different "districts" within the same city or metropolitan area; or several towns will constitute one district; or the urban high schools will be one district, whereas all the suburban nonsecondary schools will comprise a separate system; etc. To repeat, some of our "systems" involve one school; others, several. Because of certain complexities in the matching of particular teachers to their educational locales, because some teachers responded very late in the project or did not provide complete data, and because a few teachers responded as small groups, our reported data generally are based on 192 systems and 734 teachers. Especially in Questionnaires A and B, the actual *number* of respondents to a particular question varies, and is often far less than these numbers.

[6]   Harold L. Hodgkinson, *A Look at the Present.* (Washington: National Education Association, 1986)

[7]   In our Community Profile and Teacher Profile questionnaires, we asked about the level and nature of the school or system, and about the grade level of the teachers, in several different ways: name of the school or system; grade level configuration of the school and the system; grades taught by the teacher; grades at which specific subjects are taught; etc. Thus we have several bases for classification. Most secondary schools are grades 10-12 or 9-12; most elementary schools are (K)1-5 or (K)1-6, occasionally 1-8. Middle and junior high schools generally involve some pattern of grades 6-9, but there are many alternative patterns, depending on the structure of systems as a whole. With regard to these middle grades especially, ultimately we followed the classification used by the school or system,, recognizing that what is one system's "upper elementary" is another's "middle," and so on. Characterizing the *type of school* was more reliable than classifying the teaching level of individual *teachers* into three categories. Strictly speaking, when we refer to "elementary teachers" we mean those teaching in schools thus classified.

[8]   For example, there was good agreement on such classification among respondents from within the same system. Data from the level of the *district*—i.e., the community served by the schools of the district —were very similar to those from the schools.

[9]   With regard to how requirements are instituted, teachers are not the best direct source of information. For one thing, teachers tend to use the term "mandate" to mean anything they perceive as a curriculum requirement. Curriculum analysts

use it to mean something contained in educational law or regulation at some level. The latter is the usage in the table.

10 This does not automatically mean that the curriculum in social studies must vary widely across districts: for example, since teachers and administrators everywhere are aware of national trends and sentiments, the tendency that some experts predict toward an approximation to a "national curriculum" could be present in each of many or most districts.

11 The weekly national average for teaching hours is given in *Education Week*, February 7 1990.

12 The mean number of hours taught at each grade level times the number of A-R teachers reporting at that level.

13 All respondents in our study have bachelor's degrees. Of the 750 persons with bachelor's degrees who completed the question, 547 have master's degrees. Among E teachers, 105 out of 168 have the higher degree (63%); among M teachers, 138/217 (64%); among S teachers, 304/365 (83%). [Six E teachers had post-master's degrees; 8 M teachers, and 18 S teachers. Only among S teachers were there doctorates in an academic field (as opposed to Education doctorates), and these were mostly in History. These PhD or EdD degrees were so few, we have dropped them from analysis.] As a whole, our A-R teachers are quite highly educated, which might be expected from a self-selected group of this kind. The *combined* table (pp. 28) is based on 1297 separate degrees. This has the effect of retaining in the data a tally for the bachelor's field for those who have the master's. Presumably both educational experiences may have an effect on later opinions and attitudes. We emphasize that many of our teachers have many hours of course work past their highest degree; in public education it is this that determines pay differentials and professional status, not so much the possession of higher degrees per se.

14 The unweighted over-all ranks for all respondents together are the same as for S teachers, who are more numerous than E and M teachers in answering this question.

15 The first questionnaire, the *Community Profile*, was completed by one contact person representing each participating school, district, or system in the study. See p. 8.

16 It is conceivable that the wording of the question itself discouraged those who might have said, No (or little) history, just Social Science—but there is no evidence for such a view elsewhere in this study.

17 It could be that the 17.2% who stressed that all the "social sciences" were important construed the question in this way.

18 Question A7 followed the question about the "main purpose of social studies" directly; the wording of Question A7 even specified "achieving the purpose of social studies education." Some of the responses to A6 had emphasized skills that were non-subject-specific, such as critical thinking, decision-making, and the like. In the responses to A7, a number of similar responses were given, which were impossible to code in terms of named subject-matter content. It would be wrong to exclude these, since some teachers believe such skills to be content-*relevant*— i.e., that subject-matter learning counts for little without the acquisition of these skills. Accordingly, answers that dealt with these skills in clear connection with (or indistinguishable from) "content" were coded as Other, while mentions of truly basic skills, general attitudes, etc., were excluded from the data.

[19] This category separated out for this question only. For other questions in this Report, supervisors and administrators at the various levels who have teaching responsibilities are included as teachers.

[20] *Report Card on School Reform: The Teachers Speak.* Princeton, N.J.: The Carnegie Foundation for the Advancement of Teaching, 1988.

Adviser-Responder
Schools Network Members

ALABAMA: James Couch, Gary Day, Jennifer Patrick, Sue Self, Judy B. Smitherman, Jay Stejskal, Peggy Wallace

ALASKA: Lynn Divelbess, Louie Yanotti

ARKANSAS: Barbara Prather, Murphy Cauthron

ARIZONA: Steven Adolph, Ray Agee, Alfonso Aguilar, Joe Aobarsay, Dorothy Arenz, Robert Balthasar, Kathleen Barraza, Brian Black, Marvin Boyer, Carol Breyman, James Brown, Richard Brown, Ann Bruce, Michael Cady, Richard Caldwell, Larry Campbell, Cris Caufield, Anita Coppock, Adrian Cozzi, James Denton, Susan Dorsey, Lorene Ely, Richard Flanders, Wilola Follett, F. Futch, John Gentili, P. Gerlach, Mack Gilchrist, Karen Griego, Mary Lynne Glover, Thomas Goss, John Gregory, Gloria Grossman, Debra Guarnero, Judy Hackleroad, Jerry Hermanek, Patrick Herrera, Fred Johnson, Dee Johnson, Stephanie Klopper, P. Kohlhaus, Eric Ladue, P. Mandell, Gary Martinez, James McBride, J. McCarty, R. McClendon, Tom McDonald, Forrest McDonald, John Murphy, William O'Meara, Gay Parrish, Marguerite Percell, Jesus Percette, Kenneth Ridenour, C. Robinson, William Salony, J. Schmidle, Maurice Shoger, David Shores, R. Sloekess, Brenda Smith, Mack Stanley, Robert Strong, Nancy R. Stuart, Brian Tindell, Peter Tuccio, Jane Watson, Robert White

CALIFORNIA: John Beacom, Ray Dean, R. Galey, Pat Geyer, Joe Greco, Alan Haskuitz, Brent Heath, Robert Hivner, Toby Huddle, Frank Huyette, Jan Jurgemeyer, Laurie Kind, P. Koger, Ken Koury, Richard Kraft, Sam LaSalla, Margaret B. Lotz, Tim Olague, Ron Osumi, E. Robert Scrofani, Carol Sill, William Smith, Jean Topley, Tim Vargish, Jerry Walters

COLORADO: Kim Bush, James Campbell, Eileen Durneen, Kristin Early, Eilleen Ellis, Jean Gauley, Beth Gilles, Kristin Haas, Tom Johnson, Chelli Kellogg, Ted Kempton, Michael Murphy, Marcia Neal, Angie Rinaldo, Michelle Sankborn, Margaret Somerville

CONNECTICUT: Marcia Abate, Nancy Bates, Diane Beaulieu, Krista Berneike, Liz Boissard, Martha Brackeen-Harris, Deborah Brasher, Jan Lee Brookes, Robert Cox, Doug Cramphin, Jan Cusey, Robert Dilzer, Daniel Dorman, Cyndi Farquhar, Fred Fiorella, Jean Groothius, Lillian Iannone, Elizabeth Jochnick, James Ladd, Natalie Lewis, Gladys Macdonough, Charles Mann, Dierdre McCartan, Carrie O'Connor, Martha Parvis, Richard Pesce, Chris Rago, Pat Reese, Stoddard Reynolds, Carol Ridarelli, Carol Ritchie, Julie Roebelen, William Seiffert, Jeanne Selig, Maureen Stingel, Diane Sydney, Dorine Toyen, Robert Tremagton, Louise Vchaczyk, Judy Willour

DELAWARE: Michael Brelick, Stephen Hyde, P. Edward Hughs, G.A. Jackson, John O'Brien, John Morgan, Frank Singles, G. A. Stetson

DISTRICT OF COLUMBIA: Billie Day, Joseph La Blanc

FEDERAL REPUBLIC OF GERMANY (Department of Defense Schools): Joseph Bartges, Joseph Bellay, Theresa Bennett, Elizabeth Beury, Kingsley Bird, Rupert Browning, Stephen Bryant, Sandra Burdette, Anna Cadd, Michael Cardinale, Suzanne Carte, Barbara Christo, Evelyn Cornell, Ruth Cornell, Dolly Crooks, Robert Dick, Ruth Anne Diller, Caroline Dodrell, Carolyn Douglass, Martha Drane, Susan Duernberger, Phyllis Duvall, Eddy Elmore, Patrick

Fenimore, Susan Fisher, Ron Ginter, George Grantham, Carla Guthrie, Laura Hayhurst, D.B. Hedrick, Norma Herald, Cay Hoh, Nancy Hollis, Kathleen Holmes, Kathy Johnson, Mary Larson, Edward Lee, Charles Lewis, Ronald Matt, Lucille McClure, Nancy McCoy, Rose McCune, Kathleen McGee, Charles Moses, Mary Lou Myers, Barabra Navadarski, Doris Parsons, Carma Peters, Trecia Peterson, Susie Phipps, Roseann Pincus, Billie Pumphrey, Mickey Ramsey, Judith Riders, Jeanie Robinson, Todd Schwarz, Jerry Sheen, Donald Smith, Douglas Smoot, Bonnie Turner, Cindy Vargo, David Weaver, Keith Werner, Nancy White, Erma Wilson, Carolyn Withrow, Ruth Wright, Donna Wright, Nathan Yerrid

FLORIDA: Jean M. Garrison, Mary Hester, Karen Lynn, Jean McKinley, Yoshi Negora, Douglas Olafson, Joseph Saraceno, Debra Soklowski, Dan Wynn, Frank Wood

GEORGIA: Leonard Brown, Beverly King, Barbara McCay, Richard Munn

HAWAII: Rod Santos

IDAHO: Judith Myers

ILLINOIS: M. Anderson, Paul Bloomquist, Chris Butler, Douglas Chase, Marjorie Cosgrove, Sharon DiBenedetto, David Dickman, Tim Dunn, Darlene Fisher, Susanne Guyer, Tony Hogan, Deborah Johnson, Diane Kostic, Diane Leib, James Marran, Jack Mattox, Blossom Mormel, Marianne Nelson, Robert Nielson, Kathleen Rinehart, Donald Rogaw, John Sippy, William Stewart, Carolyn Sweers, Nancy Lee Van Laten, Joanne Wheeler, Barbara Wysocki

INDIANA: W. Marquis Anderson, Paul Blum, Rosemarie Bradford, Diane Brown, Marvis Jean Canon, Rosalind Fishman, Meredith E. Huston, Michael Jackson, Isabella Lindner, Thomas McGowan, Gwendolyn Mingo, Carla M. Roberts, Patricia Gannon Smith, Kathryn Stewart, Gregory Ulm, D. Young

IOWA: Al Becker, Jeff Bohlke, Mark Breitbach, Thomas Determan, Donald Fett, Judith Finkelstein, James Hantula, Tom Jenk, Janet McClain, Vincent Meis, Katie Mulholland, Oakleigh Natvig, Lynn Nielsen, Duane Nilles, John O'Connell, Dennis Oliver, Craig Olson, Joseph Ottavi, Dean Pedersen, Sr. Charmaine Plotz, Gary Potter, Tom Rawson, Harry Robbins, D.J. Ruden, Dorothy Schmaltz, Dennis Schroeder, Arden Smutzler, James Sovereign, Doug Sprague, Richard Stender, Sr. Joanne Sullivan, Robert Timmerman, Mark Topf, Evelyn Vondran, Joanne Wolfe, Judith Myers

KANSAS: Ronald Ellis, Tom Miron, Ruth Schwartz, Betty J. Thornburg, Jim Turner

KENTUCKY: Anne Aubrey, Louise Davis, John Klus, Beth Markham, Terry Miller, Minnie Pearsall

LOUISIANA: Callie Delacroix, Linda Harvison, Ferne Loupe, Barbara Mooney, Nannette Marie Murtagh, John Niemietz

MARYLAND: Robert C. Anderman, Dennis Cochran

MASSACHUSETTS: Maureen Beck, Janna Bremer, Barbara Brennan, William Brennan, Edmund Cadorette, Richard Caprio, Florence Codyer, Elizabeth Collins, R. Congleton, Regina Conley, June Coutu, John Cox, Elizabeth Cruckton, Robert Deteri, W. Dilworth, John Dwyer, Amy Ebeling, Adeline Esposito, James Jeffrey Fair, P. Gallerani, Philip Gibbons, Mary Gilmer, Ronald Godfrey, Robert Goldberg, Mary Hansen, Christine Henrich, Clarence Hoover, Lydia King Kachikurn, Virginia Keniry, Richard Kollen, Vito LaMura, Peg Madden, Mary Mahoney, Clara Manteca, William Marion, N. McMann, P. W.

Miskoff, Edward Nealon, Al Nesti, John O'Brien, John Papadonis, William Quinn, Sandy Raymond, D.S. Rogerson, Dave Secrist, Joan Sheridan, Wayne Simarrian, Prue Stuhr, T.K. Sullivan, John Tyler, Lois Valakis, Hazel Varella, Patricia Viles-Buchanan, Karen Wallstein, Waneen Winslow, Janet Youngholm, Tobi Zimmerman

MAINE: Jean Butler, Marc Gagne, Lloyd Hunt, Karol Kucinski, Arthur J. Tordoff, James Violette, Joyce Whitmore

MICHIGAN: William Argo, Pat Bailey, Patrick Brown, Jo Deshon, Martha Hawkes Drury, J. Foster, Robert Freye, Ted Garneau, Joanne Gonzalez, Pete Graham, Mikell Griffith, Rosemary Haserodt, William Hess, Michael Hemme, Donald Henson, Joan Kedlarski, Sandy Kristen, James Mikosz, Mel Miller, Myrna Myers, Judy Nevela, James Parise, Lynn Pattison, Frank Perry, Gaye Ramage, Susan Reed, David Sansing, Ronald Sartor, Nancy Schofield, Sandra Starr, Kelli Sweet, Linda Trehearne, Joanie Ugelow, Charmane Walker

MINNESOTA: Ken Jensen, Gerald Ruda, Mary Eileen Sorenson, Rick Theissen

MISSISSIPPI: Annie Archie, Anne Calvert, Harriette Elrod, Jerry Wyatt

MISSOURI: Robert Allison, Maureen Amick, Lori Brandman, Bettye Branom, Bette Bude, Dennis Chiles, Joan Coots, Gloria Dalton, Ceclia Deuser, Jacqueline Fleck, Carol Fruits, Robert Goode, Erick Hagen, Carolyn Hedrick, Lucy Henson, Paula Hopkins, Ken Jansen, Marge Jurgenson, Linda Krull, Mary MacFarland, Sandra Mawhinney, Edward Mihevc, Dianne Peters, Helena Placek, Betty Powers, Joseph Regenbogan, Ruth Schwartz, Jan Stevens, Jack Tanner, Jill Walter

MONTANA: Terry Baldus, Marilyn Ryan

NEBRASKA: Mary Allberry, Charles Gordon, William Hayes, Joseph Higgins, Isabella Linder, William Nelson, James Perry

NEVADA: Barbara Adams, Jeffrey Norris

NEW HAMPSHIRE: Philip Fujawa, Eric Herzog, David Rogacki

NEW JERSEY : Miriam Berger, William Carnathan, Dolly Cinquino, Timothy Eigo, Robert Galante, Thomas Gentile, Constance Halliwell, Carol-Ann Harris, David Kahl, Hal Kahn, J. Edward Kidd, Phillip Kinney, Abe Learner, Alan Markowitz, James Masker, Barbara Melofchek, Cindy Nealey, Joseph Pace, Joseph Petrella, James Scannelli, Allison Spatola, Karen Stollar, Hope Van den Heuvel, E. Vasile, David Whalen

NEW YORK: Cindy Beeley, John Paul Bianchi, Martin Blumenkranz, Shelia Coletta, John Culmine, Georgia Diehr, Nathan Epstein, Daniel Feldman, Peter Gaspar, Marie Goldberg, John Heintjes, JoAnn Hovey, Robert Keagle, Richard Kobliner, Haila Lehrer, A. W. Lutz, Edward Madison, Sharon Murphy, Ellen Ozer, Gale Linck Partoyan, Colin M. Ramsay, A. Reinhardt, Leonard Schiffman, Victoria Schulte, Howard Schwach, Harvey Seligman, Douglas Sheer, Robert Stenzel, Anthony Thoman, William A. Toto, Eugene Vasile, Maureen Walsh, Steve Zahurak

NORTH CAROLINA: Jeanne Boswell

NORTH DAKOTA: Robert Kulack

OHIO: Marie Blake, Vicki Baack, Dorothy Briss, Julianne Buckley, Rosemary Conroy, Lee Davis, Bob Donaldson, Graydon Doolittle, Stephen Edwards, Ann Femia, B. J. Ferriel, Andrew Fisher, Andrea Flinta, Shelly Hannah, Peggy R. Harrison, Dale Hartney, Christine Hayes, Dorene Henschen, Mary Kay Hink, Shirley Hoover, Vicki Houser, Corky Jackson, John Kingsboro, Norma Knouse, Jeanne Koehl, Jean Labuhn, Amy LaRue, Elaine Lehman, Carol Listiak, Mary

Litzinger, D. Ludlum, G. McClure, Sara McKinley, Pat Moats, Nancy Patterson, Steve Pritchett, Colin Ramsey, Sheryl Reed, Margaret Royce, Bea Sanders, Sarah Schriner, Mariruth Seubert, Marilyn Simmons, Jean Stough, Kathleen Taps, Terry Trubiano, Louise Williams, Scott Yant, Thomas Williams, Jackie Yarletts, William Ziegler

OKLAHOMA: Juli Carson, Pat Culver, Mary Lynn Hartley, Glenda LoBaugh, T. Lopis, Donna Marshall, M. Ozment, Patty Parker, Karl Springer, Stan Upchurch

OREGON: Eugene C. Bates, Jay Conroy, Judy Doyle, Peggy Freed-Elefant, John Gaskill, Peter Greco, Anne Hart, Jeryl Harrison, Dennis Hironaka, Marilyn Ismail, Jackie Miles, Thomas Ogawa, Tom Pfau, Elaine Rector, Donald Sutherland, Carrie Thompson, Van Vanelli, Earl Williams

PENNSYLVANIA: Edward Blazy, Gregory Camma, David B. Coates, William Engblom, Edward Griffith, Jacob Hoover, Arthur Jacobs, Clarence Jones, Robert McLaughlin, Thomas R. Moyer, John Newell, William Skowronski, Ruth Stas, Robert Stratton, T. R. Tabor

RHODE ISLAND: Richard Dubois

SOUTH CAROLINA: Edward A. Ahrens, Sr., Kathy Amick, Gil Baco, Shirley Fry, Mary Lou Gruel, Elijah Heyward, Kathryn Kihn, Nancy Lynn, Ursula Marcier, Teresa Rounds, Phillip Sheppard, Roy Stehle, Victoria Wolf

SOUTH DAKOTA: Marsha Bruning, Kelly Gillkyson, Mary Lea Hennies, Mary Johnson, Allen Kosters, Joyce Zimmer

TENNESSEE: Mel Brown, Carmon Mae Brown, Connnie Frensley Delaney, Louise Osborne, Dorine Toyen

TEXAS: Dick Alston, Michelle Arledge, Jean Babcock, Linda Black, Royce Black, Kathy Breazeale, Jo Bristow, Enid Butler, Michelle Caton, Linda Chancellor, Bill Chilivetis, Carolyn Churchwell, Sherion Clark, Jack Comming, M. S. Copple, Avis Crisp, Lisa Crow, Lisa Currie, Jan K. Dean, Mike Dennis, Lou De Santiago, Mary Ellen Emery, Randy Farr, Nadine Fidler, Pat Flatt, Jon Ford, Linda Francis, Debbie Garner, Herbert Gehring, Thomas Gothia, Kay Goud, Nancy Graves, Nancy Greene, Margaret Hamilton, Sherry Harper, Jackie Helmes, Sherry Henderson, Carolyn Hodges, Donna Holmes, John Mark Honea, Cathy Jackson, Charles Jehlan, Alyson Johnson, Rodney Karr, Sidney Kerr, Thomas Kroutter, Carol Kuykendall, Carol Lawrence, Jane Lee, Becky Lucas, Freida McArthur, Lauri McNally, Glen McNath, Julia Monks, Annelle Moody, Douglas Morris, Christine Morrison, Tom Newman, Bonnie Northcutt, Phil Pate, Jack Porter, Randy Porter, Linda Reeves, Gail Riley, Edith Roberts, Mike Rogers, James Salinas, Paul Sample, Jo Sekalym, Gayla Shannon, Christina Shahan, Jean Slaydon, Mary Smith, Norma Sturdivant, Eileen Thomas, Juliann Warner, Dan Washmon, Carolyn Waters, Sid Weinman, Pam Wells, Willie Williams, Helen Wilson, Michael Wood, Loyce Wukasch, Jimmy Wyble

UTAH: Bill Clark, Jim Fuller, Norma Jean Remington, Claudia Seiter, David Seiter, Joe Spendlove

VERMONT: Barry Aldinger, Alan Blakeman, Pamela Brown, Ronald Dustin Nimblett, Albert Pitt, Roberta Steponaitis, Sandy Stoddert, Jon Yarnell

VIRGINIA: Suzanne AuCoin, Alan Blakeman, Carole Bouthilet, Nancy Brown, Davis Chung, Don Cooper, K.Coston, Susan Demeria, Lelia Ermarth, Holly Frazier, Carolyn Gecan, Judy Gibson, Peter Gredler, Susan Gredler, Louise Holley, Alison Hughes, Karen Korcel, Jerry Landis, Brigitte Lavey, J. E. Lloyd, Meggie Long, Karen Lucas, Janet Martin, Connie Mauck, Mary McDiarmid, M.

Mercando, Barbara O'Byrne, Ron Patterson, H. M. Pearson, Virginia Reed, Carolyn Reilly, David Ruffo, Judy Schlim, Ray Schupp, Seymour Stiss, Angelica Suddeth, Judith C. Williams, James Wilson

WASHINGTON: Alice Alcorn, Shirley Callaway, Katrina Dohn, Bob Elmer, Donna Kontos, Dick Fain, Gladys Libolt, Kathy Luksan, E. Morris, Pat Watson

WEST VIRGINIA: Lois Bailey, Lynn Barnes, Delbert Brannon, Joe Cielensky, Linda Conley, Joseph Craffey, Sherry Dietrich, Sue Goodwin, Ronald Ginter, Dortha Hedrick, Elizabeth Howard, Sharon Isringhaus, Kathy Johnson, M. Larson, Robert Neely, Sandra Puckett, Linda Poff, Mary Thornton, Betty Wagner, Ann Wells, Calvin Whitteker, Werner, Gayle Wise, Vicki Wood, Donna Wright

WISCONSIN: James Brown, Barbara Erdman, James Grinsel, James Havlish, Sharon Hough, Mary Jarvis, James Kraft, Dianne Kretz, Mike McKinnon, Scott Miles, Kathleen Morris, Neil Munson, Henry Osswald, Henry Pleuss, Jean Schollmeier, Allan Solomonson

WYOMING: Susanne Hayden, Donald Morris.

We also thank those teachers who submitted questionnaires without names.

Notes

Notes

Notes

Notes

Notes

Notes

Notes

DATE DUE
